WHEN YOU CAN'T
SNAP
OUT OF IT

WHEN YOU CAN'T
SNAP
OUT OF IT

Finding
YOUR WAY
THROUGH
DEPRESSION

LOUIS J.BEVILACQUA, PSY. D.

YorkshirePublishing
www.yorkshirepublishing.com
Write Now.

ISBN: 978-1-947491-27-4
When You Can't Snap Out of It
Copyright © 2011 by Louis J. Bevilacqua PSY. D.

Yorkshire Publishing
3207 South Norwood Avenue
Tulsa, Oklahoma 74135
www.YorkshirePublishing.com
918.394.2665

DEDICATION

This book is dedicated to all of the individuals who have taught me what works in trying to manage or overcome the symptoms of depression. Most importantly, this book is for those who are still struggling. I want you to know, there is hope for healing.

ACKNOWLEDGMENTS

This is my first self-help book, and the experience was very different than my previous books for professional audiences. For years I thought about writing this book but just never did it. When I finally put some ideas down on paper I ran it by a trusted colleague Frank Dattilio, Ph.D., ABPP. Frank is one of the leading figures in the world in cognitive-behavior therapy and my co-author for two other professional books (*Comparative Treatments for Relationship Dysfunction*, by Springer Publishing, and *The Brief Family Therapy Homework Planner 2nd Ed.*, by Wiley & Sons). It was Frank who supported my efforts and encouraged me to take the risk on writing this book. He also provided invaluable insight into some of the content of this book. For your continued support, I am tremendously grateful. Thanks, Frank. Another colleague was one of my pre-doctoral interns, Keith Milligan. Keith was very interested in my work and wanted to help out. Thanks to Keith the appendix section on depression diagnoses was written. You did a great job, Keith—thanks. Tom Whiteman, Ph.D., is the founder of Life Management Services, which incorporates three companies: Life Counseling Services, Rehab After Work/After School, and the Light Program. Tom developed the Life Counseling Services Depression Screen and was gracious enough to grant me permission to use it in this book—thanks, Tom. A special thanks goes to Dr.'s Edward McGonigle, Misook Soh and John J. Thomas for helping review the medication charts in the chapter, "Common Medications Used To Treat Depression." Since this is a self-help book geared for the general public, I thought it might be best to get some feedback from people I respect and who are not in the therapy field. To my wife, Debbie Bevilacqua; my sister, Lori Dafilou; and my sister-in-law, Shelby Bird, thank you for indulging me and taking the time to review my work. I appreciate your insight and excellent suggestions. I also ran portions of the manuscript by several clients, who are the real experts on what works. After their approval, the manuscript was handed off to Tate Publishing. The staff at Tate was fabulous. Special thanks goes to Sheridan Irick my conceptual editor. Sheridan made sure this was a top-notch manuscript. Kristen Verser did an outstanding job on the cover design. Special thanks also goes to Rachael Sweeden and Janey Hays who believed in the book from the beginning.

TABLE OF CONTENTS

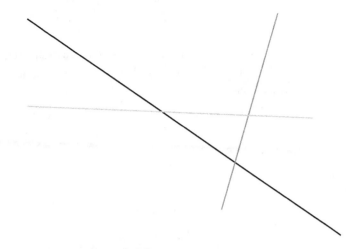

INTRODUCTION

No one wants to be depressed. Unfortunately, depression affects millions of us every day. There are numerous reasons why we get depressed. Perhaps we experience a trauma in our lives. Perhaps something bad happens such as losing a job or relationship. Perhaps someone we love passes away. Maybe we feel alone or uncared for. Maybe we have a very limited support group. Or perhaps the people we believe are our support group aren't very supportive! Maybe we don't think very highly of ourselves and have low self-esteem. Sometimes we can't point to any specific reason for why we feel depressed. We may have everything we need in life. A good home, nice family life, good health and we still feel depressed. Some people will tell us to "just get over it" or "just snap out of it." Such individuals usually don't understand depression or what it is really like to be depressed. Their suggestions, although perhaps well-intentioned, are of little help.

When you are depressed, you tend to think:

- *I feel so empty inside.*

- *I just don't care.*

- *All I want to do is sleep.*

- *I don't like anything anymore.*

- *I don't have the energy to do anything.*

- *I'm just not hungry.*

- *I'm useless.*

- *I'm worthless.*

- *I can never do anything right.*

- *I'm such a loser.*

- *Things will never work out for me.*

- *Life's not worth it.*

- *I sometimes think I'd be better off dead.*

- *Nobody cares.*

If you identified with any of the comments listed above, chances are you are struggling with some level of depression. If you would like to measure your depression I would encourage you to take the Life Counseling Services (LCS) Depression Screening listed in the appendix. You could also repeat the screening over the next several weeks as you read this book. Your scores will serve as sort of a thermometer. As your score goes down, so will your feeling of depression.

Depression, like all emotions, is a normal part of living. Some days are better than others. Some days you may feel okay, and other days you may feel really depressed. For clarification purposes, let's differentiate depression from feeling down.

When you are depressed, you tend to think that things will not work out or it will be next to impossible for the situation to change or improve. When you are depressed, you have very little energy and oftentimes prefer to be alone. Events that used to be of interest to you no longer seem to have purpose for you. Your appetite and sleep patterns may be different than usual. In particular, you tend to think in negative terms about yourself, your situation, and your future. You might be feeling so bad that you feel guilty and worthless and may even contemplate suicide. To be diagnosed with depression, the symptoms just described need to be present more often than not for at least two weeks and must interfere with your life. There are many different types and levels of depression. To read about the criteria for various diagnoses of depression see Appendix B: Depression Diagnoses.

When you are feeling down you feel "blah." You don't really want to do much. You are probably quiet and keeping more to yourself. Your appetite might be different than usual. You may feel bad about your situation or about yourself. However, you most likely are not feeling worthless, hopeless, or suicidal.

The primary difference has to do with the level of intensity, duration, and whether the symptoms are interfering with your ability to function (i.e. at work, at home, or in school) on a regular basis.

Usually if you have been feeling down, after a short period of time (i.e. few hours or a day or two) you start to bounce back. Your outlook on your situation starts to change. You get back to doing things and you re-engage with life. If the struggle continues for more than a couple weeks with little or no relief, you are more than likely experiencing some form of depression.

If so, you're not alone, and, like many others, you are probably trying to figure out why!

To identify why we are feeling depressed is important because it gives us a sense of understanding. When we can explain why, we tend to feel better to some degree. It makes us feel more like everyone else and less of an outcast. Being able to explain why we are feeling a certain way also gives us some sense of sanity. It feels better to be able to say, "This is what I am feeling, and this is why." Sometimes, however, we feel depressed and don't know why. We may have some explanation, but it's not enough for us. After a while, the "why" becomes less important, and the focus turns to ending the depression. We want to stop feeling depressed.

This book was written to describe a vast array of options for how to manage and even overcome various symptoms of depression. There are exercises in this book for everyone. There will be exercises for those who like to write, read, or be more hands on and physical. Some will be simple and others a little more challenging. Throughout the book you will read short descriptions of how people struggling with the symptoms of depression describe their experience. (The names have been changed to protect confidentiality.) The strategies and suggestions are based on what these individuals have done to feel better. Depression does not have to control you. These exercises can help you regain control of who you want to be and how you would like to act.

There are three essential goals to reading this book.

1. To understand the different levels of depression and how multiple factors contribute to feeling depressed.

2. To realize that you are not alone.

3. To learn and develop a resource of options *you can* use to manage or overcome the symptoms of depression.

What you will gain from reading this book:

a. To understand how taking charge of what you do and how you think can enable you to have the feelings you want.

b. The benefits of accepting what you can control *and* what you cannot.

c. What you need to do in order to take time to be an observer of yourself.

d. To identify the benefits of living by your values instead of living by how you feel.

e. To understand the role that patterns or cycles play in your life.

f. By understanding how something happens we can also learn to change it.

g. How to utilize a problem solving formula.

What you will *not* get from reading this book:

a. A lot of references from or for other books to read.

b. A bunch of statistics or research findings.

c. A list of labels to stick on yourself and define what you are.

d. Accounts of people who are happy telling you how to be like them.

HOW TO USE THIS BOOK

This book is intended for you to relate to other people and to learn or be reminded of what you *can do* about feeling depressed. In reading it you will realize that we *all* struggle with our feelings! When you feel depressed it's tough to concentrate and think clearly about what to do. This book is designed to be a quick reference guide and resource of exercises and options on what to do. Some exercises may be more helpful than others. Everyone is different, so it is important to have lots of options. What works for one person may not work for someone else. Sometimes a strategy may work for you this week but not the next. The more options you have, the more prepared and better equipped you are to beat depression. Read it and reread it. Practice the suggestions even if you don't believe in them at first. Begin to increase the use of the suggestions in your daily life. Many of the suggestions involve writing lists or responding to questions. Therefore, I strongly encourage you to use a journal or notebook while reading through the book. This will help you to track, add to, and make changes to your answers over time. If at any time you begin to experience a symptom of depression, you can easily glance at the table of contents to find the symptom or symptoms you are struggling with. Once you identify which symptom(s) you need support to manage, just turn to that chapter, and review the options. If you struggle with all the symptoms described, and many people do, then just start at the beginning. You can use this book while in therapy as an adjunct resource. It can also be used for those individuals who are not in therapy but have identified certain symptoms of depression that you want to manage or overcome.

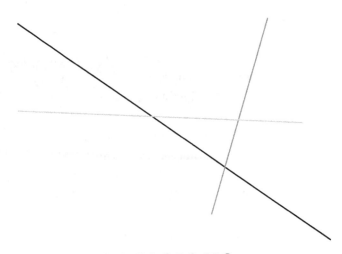

WHAT IS DEPRESSION?
HOW DEPRESSED AM I?

If you ask a therapist or psychiatrist, "What is depression?" you are most likely going to hear the criteria listed in the *Diagnostic and Statistical Manual for Mental Disorders IV-TR* (DSM). Based on the DSM, there are several different forms of depression ranging from an Adjustment Disorder with Depressed Mood to Major Depressive Disorder. To be diagnosed with some form of depression a person must meet a certain number of criteria for a certain period of time, and his or her social or occupational functioning must be negatively affected. For a more descriptive list of diagnoses and criteria for depression you can go to Appendix B: Depression Diagnoses.

If you ask people who experience depression they are unlikely to cite the DSM. Instead they will describe depression as the following:

> "I just don't feel like doing anything or believe that I can do anything. I'm just so tired and have no energy. Nothing really interests me anymore. Everything is just boring to me. I just don't care that much."

> "I just feel so bad. It hurts. I cry, and sometimes feel like I'll never stop crying."

> "When I feel depressed, I sleep and just don't want to be around anyone. I go to work, come home, say hi—maybe I'll eat something and then right to bed I go. Only to wake up the next day and do it again."

> "Everything is just negative. I can't get out of my head. The thoughts are awful. Nothing is good. It gets so bad that I don't even know what the point is anymore."

In order to gauge your level of depression, take a moment to complete the Life Counseling Services Depression Screening in Appendix A. This will also be a way for you to monitor and track your level of depression. As you take the screening from time to time, you will most likely see slightly different scores. This helps in allowing you to recognize that the intensity and level of feelings change. All feelings are transient. They come and go and fluctuate over time. That is good to understand since depression can sometimes feel like it never leaves or lessens.

For anyone who experiences depression, life can be quite a challenge. A question often asked is how do feelings occur? Feelings occur in all kinds of ways. There is no one way that anyone of us can say, "This is it. This is how a feeling occurs." What we do know is that our thoughts and behaviors play a major role in how we will feel. To demonstrate, let's refer to Loretta's story:

LORETTA

When someone recently hit Loretta's car and didn't even leave a note, she was ticked off and frustrated. She slammed her car door after getting a towel out to try and wipe off the bumper mark from the other car. Loretta thought about how bad her car looked and that it was probably going to cost a lot to repair it. She worried about it being a lease and how the dealership was going to make her pay when she traded it back in. As Loretta drove to her office, she was gritting her teeth and clenching her fists. All of these thoughts and behaviors that Loretta was engaging in only served to reinforce her feelings of anger and frustration. Once she arrived at her office, Loretta started to realize that she needed to calm down and change her feelings because she would be seeing colleagues in a meeting in a few minutes. Knowing that she needed to be present and attentive in the meeting, she started to relax her shoulders and back, telling herself, *It's just a car. I'll get it fixed soon and it will look great. Things like this happen! It's not the end of the world. My car still rides beautifully.* When Loretta walked into her office suite, she began chatting with some of her staff, put her things down in her office, and started checking messages. Loretta started to feel calm and looked forward to her first meeting that day.

As you can see, Loretta's feelings changed because of many reasons. Time had passed. She was no longer looking at her car and focusing on the damage or the misfortune she had experienced. Loretta had physically started to relax her body. She changed her context and environment by going inside. She was talking to others and thinking about other things—things that were not upsetting or aggravating. In looking over this example, you can see how internal and external factors played a role in how Loretta was feeling. Take note that she only had control over what she was actually thinking about and her behavior. These are referred to as internal factors.

We are more in control of internal factors such as our thoughts, emotions, and behaviors than we are in control of external factors. External factors would include family life, relationships, employment and school satisfaction, friendships, finances, housing, the weather, etc. We have very little if any control over them. For example, have you ever felt overwhelmed by all that is expected of you at work? Have you ever felt like you would never be able to catch up and do it all? Another external factor is our home life. Have you ever felt exhausted from cleaning up the house after everyone—all the time! Or felt fed up with having to drive the kids to their fifty million different activities or friends' houses? How about feeling upset over the bills or what you want to buy but can't afford? Or does the state of the economy have you stressed?

Such life circumstances can make life seem pretty harsh. Another external factor is family life. How difficult and tiring is it to raise children as a single parent? How about being married but having a spouse who is more often than not working or unavailable? Or raising a child with special needs? How about living with little or no support system? There are numerous other external factors that could be described, and I am sure you could contribute to that list. However, the point is that what we experience on a day-to-day basis can reinforce how we feel.

Although the external factors are outside of our control, how we respond to such situations or happenings has to do with the internal factors such as our thoughts, perceptions, and beliefs about life situations. These internal factors are sometimes even more troubling than the external ones. At least we can leave the office, classroom, or house sometimes. Leaving our thoughts is another story—possible, but still another story.

Our brains produce thoughts all the time. Imagine the New York stock exchange ticker as our brains. Imagine all the stock reports that are constantly running across the board as our thoughts running across our mind.

We are interested in some of the stocks because we may have investments in them. We pay little if any attention to the ones we have not invested. The same can be said for our thoughts. Some thoughts we pay a lot of attention to and others not so much. For example, if you struggle with feeling good about yourself, you are likely to pay more attention to thoughts that remind you of or reinforce the belief "I'm not that good" or "I'm not good enough." Throughout the day you probably tune in to similar thoughts that are negative or that minimize your self-worth. When situations occur that reinforce "I'm not good enough," you might say, "See? That's why I'm not good enough." For example, you might make a mistake. "Oh, no! I messed up. Why do I always do that?" In other words we can always find evidence to support our beliefs. When we find such evidence we focus on it. This makes us feel congruent with our beliefs. For example, if we don't believe we are very attractive and someone gives us a compliment, we are likely to dismiss it or minimize it. We may say, "You're just saying that." We may just deny it flat out: "No I'm not." That might be because that thought doesn't agree with our belief. This is also why it is tough to change thoughts about ourselves because they contradict our beliefs. It is our belief system that tends to run our lives. We tend to do things we believe are right. When we do something we believe is wrong it creates internal conflict. If we believe we are not pretty or not smart, we will dismiss or deny information that tries to negate it. For example, you might be thinking, *This book is too simple,* or *It doesn't make sense.* If that's what you believe, you will want to put it down and stop reading. In doing so, your behavior will be matching your belief system. If, on the other hand, you agree with it or get what is being described, you are likely to keep reading.

As you may have guessed, our thoughts (T), behaviors (B), and feelings (F) are inter-connected and each one influences the other. See Figure 1.A.

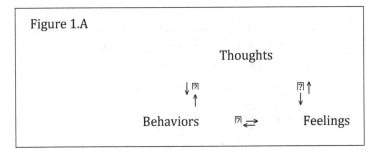

Figure 1.A

Thoughts

Behaviors ⇄ Feelings

Sometimes we behave or do something like lose our keys (B) and think, *How dumb of me* (T). Then we feel stupid (F). Sometimes we think, *I can't do that* (T), and we avoid (B) trying, so then we feel disappointed (F) in ourselves. Sometimes we feel down (F), so we don't get out of the house (B) and run those errands and then we think, *I can't do it* (T). There are many examples that demonstrate the relationship between our thoughts, feelings, and behaviors. The bottom line is that each one influences the other. This is important to know if you want to change how you feel or learn to accept how you feel. In the example above regarding losing your keys and feeling stupid, you can ask yourself, "Do I want to feel stupid?"

This may sound silly, but is it truly what you want? If not, what can you do about it? Ask yourself, "How do I want to feel?" We do have a choice as to how we feel about things. The same can be asked regarding feeling depressed. My guess is that you don't want to feel the way you do, or you wouldn't have selected this book. However, are you willing to try some things to make that happen? If the answer is yes, keep reading. The remainder of this book is about listing various symptoms of depression. You may relate to some or all of these symptoms.

For each symptom identified there will be several strategies that you will be able to try out. Many of the tools will be ones you have heard about before. If so, then this book can serve as a reminder or resource for you. Perhaps other strategies will be new or will be explained with a little twist to what you have heard before. In either case the goal of this book is to provide you with a quick reference for what you can do to manage or even overcome your symptoms of depression.

THE COGNITIVE MODEL OF CONCEPTUALIZING DEPRESSION

One of the most noticeable aspects of this book is the emphasis on our thoughts and how our thoughts are a crucial influencing factor to our feelings. You'll notice that most of the exercises or strategies involve looking at your thoughts, challenging your thoughts, and changing your thoughts. The reason for this is that the majority of the exercises, as well as the conceptualization of this book, is based on cognitive therapy as developed by Aaron Beck, M.D. Cognitive therapy is one of the most effective and powerful forms of psychotherapy today. There is an abundance of empirical studies demonstrating the effectiveness of cognitive therapy in the treatment of numerous disorders such as major depression, generalized anxiety, social phobia, obsessive-compulsive disorder, substance abuse, and eating disorders as well as many medical conditions. Cognitive therapy has been applied around the world to couples, families, children, adolescents, and adults. The overwhelming number of studies demonstrating how cognitive therapy helps individuals develop hope, motivation, purpose, and to feel better as well as my personal experience in working with clients is why this book is being written with such an emphasis on cognitive therapy. The bottom line is because cognitive therapy works!

The principles of cognitive therapy are quite simple. However, don't let that fool you. The key is in understanding how these principles play a role in your everyday life. Once you develop that understanding you must then actively work on applying the strategies in this book to make the necessary changes. Keep in mind that in order to change your current situation you must take an active and willing role in changing it. (Even if you don't currently believe it can change.)

Before you hear about what you need to do, let me explain the three primary principles of cognitive therapy in order to give you a brief understanding of the theory behind the strategies and exercises.

Cognitive or *cognition* essentially refers to our thoughts. The basis of cognitive therapy is that our thoughts greatly influence our feelings. Imagine this. You and a friend are watching a sports game. You like one team, and your friend likes the other team. At the end of the game one team is a winner, and the other is a loser. If your team is the winner, you will most likely feel happy. Your friend, on the other hand, will feel sad. Why? Since your team won, you are probably thinking and saying things like, "Yeah! All right! Way to go! My team is great." All of these are very positive thoughts and exclamations. Your friend, on the other hand, is probably having very different thoughts going through his mind. Although this may sound like a very simplistic view, it is still very accurate in explaining why you feel happy and your friend feels sad or disappointed or even angry. Feelings are influenced by how we think about, perceive, or interpret a situation. Feelings about ourselves are influenced by how we think about ourselves. If I think I'm a loser or worthless, then I'm going to feel pretty bad. Now you might be thinking, *Oh, so you're saying just think happy thoughts, and I won't be depressed?* No, I'm not. If it was that easy you wouldn't be reading this book, and I wouldn't be writing it. Remember, I said the principles were an easy concept. The key is applying them. That is the challenge.

The cognitive model or theory of depression is rooted primarily in three principles: the cognitive triad, schemas, and thinking errors. The cognitive triad refers to how a person views herself, her daily life experiences, and her future. As you might guess, if a person views herself, her daily life, and her future in a negative way she is most likely pretty depressed. For example, Vicky is a twenty-two-year-old recent college graduate. She lives at home and is applying for jobs in her field of communications. Vicky has had three interviews, one second interview, and no job offers after two months of searching for a job. She sees her situation as hopeless. She believes she will be stuck living with her parents forever, and it is all because she is a terrible person with no likeable qualities. Vicky is obviously interpreting her situation as quite negative and sees herself as defective. Vicky has struggled with depression since the age of fifteen. For Vicky to see things in less negative terms is quite difficult. When anyone is depressed there is a very good chance that they are seeing themselves, their situation and/or their future from a pessimistic or hopeless viewpoint.

The second principle involves the concept of schemas. Schemas are rules or beliefs that a person uses to live his or her life. More simply put, schemas are the core beliefs we hold regarding ourselves, the world around us, and people in general. We use schemas to evaluate, categorize, make sense of, and explain our experiences. These schemas or core beliefs are developed in childhood as we interact with significant others and experience situations. It is probably safe to say that all of us have both positive and negative schemas. In keeping with our example, Vicky may have a schema or belief about herself such as "I'm not capable" or "I need others to help me." Her schema or belief regarding people might be, "People are supposed to be helpful," or "People don't like me." Sometimes when we are pretty depressed we might have a schema or belief that people don't care. In regard to the future, Vicky may have the schema or belief "Things never seem to work out for me." We often focus selectively on information that reinforces our core beliefs, and we tend to discount or disregard information that is to the contrary. That is how these beliefs become so entrenched over time. These beliefs become so strong that they become the way we believe things to be in the world. And because that's the "way it is," we behave accordingly. So if we believe that people are not to be trusted, we will behave very cautiously and keep people at a distance, making it hard for them to get close to us. We will be reluctant to let our guard down and be vulnerable.

The third principle involves cognitive distortions or what is often referred to as thinking errors. We all engage in many thinking errors all the time. It is these thinking errors that influence our behavioral reactions and our emotional reactions to things. Take a look at the list below and see which of the common distorted and irrational thinking patterns you relate to.

- All-or-Nothing Thinking: This is when you view things in extreme terms. You are either good or bad. You have trouble seeing the gray areas. Some people who see things in such a manner are perfectionists. *If I don't get a job that means I'm a loser.*

- Catastrophizing or Fortune Telling: This is when you look at the future and predict that bad things will happen without considering alternative outcomes. You make things out to be worse than they really are. *I'm never going to get out of my parents' house.*

- Mind Reading: This is when you believe you know what others are thinking. *They're not going to hire me.*

- Dark Glasses or Mental Filtering: This is when you block out the positives and just focus on the negatives. For example, Vicky's last semester grades were three As, one B, and one D. When she found out Vicky thought, *I am so dumb I got a D.*

- Personalizing: This is when you take on the responsibility for something that is not your fault or is outside of your control. Vicky might be thinking, *No one is going to call me for a job because my resumé is poorly written or because I must have been an awful interviewee.* Vicky is only looking at her being the problem instead of also exploring the poor economic situation we are in or other plausible factors.

- Discounting: This is when you reject the positive things that happen to you. For example, Vicky has had three first interviews and one second interview. None of her friends have been offered even one interview. Vicky thinks, *I might have had a few interviews, but I still don't have a job offer.*

- Double Standard: This is when you hold yourself to a different standard than you would a friend. It's easier to give someone else a break, but you have to be perfect.

- Woulda, coulda, shoulda Statements: This is another way of putting yourself down and criticizing yourself more than necessary. You may also find fault with the world or others unnecessarily. *I should have spent more time on my resumé. I should have been more upbeat in that interview.*

If you are like most people, you were able to relate to at least a few of these thinking errors!

When you combine having thinking errors like those just described with a negative belief system and a negative view of yourself, situation, and the future, you get depression.

So what does all this have to do with managing or overcoming my symptoms of depression? Well, in order to change something it is important to understand how something works. Cognitive therapists believe that our feelings of depression and anxiety are greatly influenced by our thoughts and belief patterns. If you accept that and understand how your thoughts and beliefs influence your level of depression, then changing such thoughts and beliefs will change your level of depression. Makes sense right? Now comes the hard part—how?

Keep in mind that depression, like any emotion, is a state of being. Therefore, it is time limited. We cannot sustain the same intensity level of any feeling forever. It has to lessen at some point. This is because life is ever changing. Things are happening all the time. The weather changes, time keeps ticking.

In order to change it is important to identify what the end result of that change might look like once you achieve it. Imagine being an artist and being asked to draw a portrait of someone. It helps to picture what that person looks like in order to complete that portrait.

Try looking at your situation as being on a continuum. If one end of the continuum is total despair and hopelessness and the other end is total joy and happiness, where are you today? Where do you want to be in two weeks? Two months? Six months?

If you want to feel better and less depressed what would that look like? How would you be acting around the house? How would you be interacting with others? Would you be interacting with others? Would you be out of the house? Would you be engaging in hobbies or activities of your liking? Would you be working? What kinds of thoughts would you be focusing on about yourself? Your situation? Your future?

Sometimes, however, we don't know what that change should look like. One thing to do is to identify what you don't want it to look like. Once you do that, try and describe the exact opposite. For example your depression might look like the following:

DEPRESSION:	THE OPPOSITE:
Little or no energy	Doing a couple activities each day
Thinking poorly of yourself	Identifying one or more positives about yourself
Isolating and avoiding interactions	Getting together/ contacting someone
Feeling hopeless/helpless	Identifying some of your positive capabilities/ accomplishments

The remaining chapters are based on the primary symptoms often described by people who struggle with depression. For each symptom, numerous ideas, strategies, and options are offered. There is also a chapter on common medications used to treat depression.

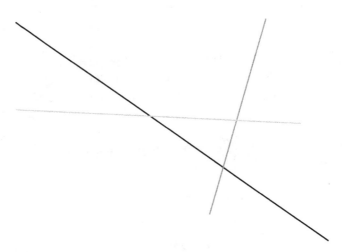

NEGATIVE THOUGHTS:

"LIFE IS TOO MUCH; IT'S AWFUL. I CAN'T ... "

Debbie works full time as a stay-at-home mom. On a daily basis, Debbie deals with negative thoughts running through her mind. These thoughts typically involve some sort of putdown regarding her self-worth. Whenever she and her son have an argument, Debbie will criticize herself and think that she is doing an awful job as a mom. If she doesn't cook dinner one night, she thinks of herself as lazy. Some thoughts Debbie replays in her mind are:

> *I'm too tired to keep trying.*
>
> *I can't do this.*
>
> *I'm such an incompetent and stupid parent.*
>
> *There is something fundamentally wrong/broken about me.*

Stacy is out of work. She lives with her cat and two dogs. Stacy describes struggling with trusting others. She has been burned before and believes it is easier to keep to herself without letting others get too close. When anyone tries, she starts to think, *What do they really want?* Some of the thoughts Stacy has include:

> *No one really cares about me.*
>
> *I'm not worth caring about.*
>
> *Life is just too hard.*
>
> *I'm scared.*
>
> *It's better to be alone.*

Negative thoughts can become so overwhelming it can feel like they control our lives. Even when we think about our thoughts we can say they don't make logical sense, but they *feel* so true! Sometimes we have said them and heard them so many times we find it hard to believe anything else.

What if you did think and eventually believed something else? How might that affect your level of depression?

The idea of thinking in terms of "what if…" is a strategy you can use to change or alter negative thought patterns. In order to alter or change negative thoughts you need to identify other thoughts you could focus on. To do this, use your journal or notebook. On the left side of the page record some of the negative thoughts you typically have running through your mind, and on the right side of the page generate more reassuring and positive alternative thoughts. This may not be as easy as it sounds. Some people report that listing the negative side is easy, but the right side takes more time and thought. You can enlist the help of any person with whom you feel comfortable. Use Debbie's sample chart below to give yourself a start.

"WHAT ELSE CAN I THINK?"

Table 3.A Negative Thoughts – Alternative Thoughts

Negative Thoughts	Alternative/Positive Thought
I'm such an incompetent/stupid parent.	Parenting is the hardest job in the world. All parents are human and make mistakes. There are lots of times I've been a great parent. (Try to think of a time you did something and your child smiled as a result)
I'm not worth caring about.	I am worth caring about because I do a lot for my kids. I drive them to their activities and friend's houses. I care for their physical health. I give them love and affection. (Take a moment to remind yourself of the things you do as a parent)
Life is just too hard. I can't do this anymore.	Life is sometimes hard especially when I feel overwhelmed. If I reduce my expectations and focus on one realistic goal for today life will feel easier and a little more manageable.

As you know, negative thoughts get into our heads and don't want to leave. We can focus on and entertain such thoughts for hours, days, weeks, and even longer. If that happens to you then you might like the following idea. It involves staying in your head and using your imagination to some degree. It can also be brought to life and played out for real. It's called "The Courtroom."

"THE COURTROOM"

Imagine that you are in a courtroom. You are going to pretend to be both the defense attorney and prosecutor. The negative thoughts (i.e. *I'm worthless* or *I'm not good enough*) are on trial. As the defense attorney you are to create an argument for why the negative thoughts are true. This is typically quite easy for people feeling depressed or who struggle with thinking positive. The negative thoughts and times we "messed up" are easily recalled. As the prosecutor you have to prove the negative thoughts are false and should be sent to prison. This part might prove more challenging. You will need to find evidence to support and negate the negative thoughts. You can bring witnesses such as people who care about you. Think of those who appreciate you. You can have a jury of your friends and support network. Or, you can just have a judge. The judge is *you*. Once you hear both sides, as the judge you must make a ruling. If the negative thoughts are to go to prison be sure to imagine them leaving and being handcuffed as they are taken away.

Sometimes thoughts keep playing over and over again and never seem to have an off button. What can be useful is an interruption that causes you to snap out of being in your head and listening to those negative thoughts. Review the list below and see what you can add to it in order to "snap out of it."

"SNAP OUT OF IT"

1. Put a rubber band around your wrist and snap it. (Caution: Do not do this to the point of breaking your skin or causing pain!)

2. Clap you hands as loud as you can.

3. Scream STOP either out loud or just in your head.

4. Turn on music and put headphones or earphones on.

5. Slam a book down on a desk or tabletop.

6. Picture a stop sign or perhaps make one to physically see.

7. Change the channel on the radio or a musical CD that you are listening to as a physical representation of changing your focus or thoughts.

8. In your journal, rewrite the above list and add as many other ideas as you can.

Usually attempts to "snap out of it" need to be paired with a behavioral strategy as well. The "snapping out of it" tool is primarily to increase your conscious awareness to the fact that you are overly focusing on the negative thoughts running through your mind. In order to be successful you will most likely need to physically engage in some kind of activity. Review the list of options below and add some of your own ideas:

"WHAT TO DO INSTEAD"

1. Call a friend.

2. Go for a walk outside.

3. Go talk to someone near you.

4. Go get a coffee/tea/soda from a convenience store or bookstore.

5. Go to a mall and walk around.

6. Go watch a movie or TV show.

7. Go read a book.

8. Go draw, paint, or sculpt something.

9. Put this list in your journal and leave room to add more ideas over the next few weeks.

Notice that each idea starts with the word *go!* Individuals who engage in a physical activity are more likely to report a decrease in depressive symptoms than those who don't.

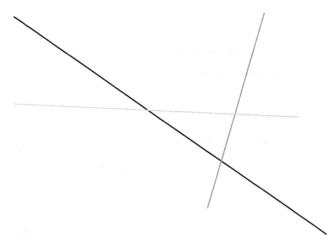

ISOLATING:

"I'M SO ALONE. WHERE'S THE SUPPORT?"

Lisa is a twenty-five-year-old woman. She works as a nurse on the third shift. She lives alone and had a boyfriend for the past six months. Since age thirteen she has felt depressed. Lisa often feels that no one understands. She thinks that her friends have to be tired of hearing about her depression.

Matt is a thirty-three-year-old man who is married and has two kids. He describes his wife as sarcastic and says she "doesn't have a sympathetic bone in her body." When he tries to talk about feeling down, his wife tells him stop being so negative, "Look at all you have to be happy about," she says.

Alice is a forty-six-year-old married woman and mother of two teenagers. She feels unreal and disconnected from people. Sometimes support can be overwhelming: "It's too intense, too much pressure."

Another symptom of depression is isolating yourself. Sometimes you isolate yourself because the depression makes you want to be alone. Other times, you might not have any people who know how to support you. Perhaps you have a hard time trusting others, so you don't want to reach out. Maybe you believe that asking for help is a sign of weakness. Whatever the reason, isolating tends to reinforce or maintain a sense of depression. As a result the larger goal would be to increase social interaction. How to do that can be rather difficult.

There are lots of ways to reach out and re-engage with people.

"WAYS TO CONNECT"

1. E-mail

2. Facebook

3. Text

4. Phone call

5. Letter

6. Leave your room and go to the kitchen or living room

7. Get that journal out again. Here's another opportunity to add to your toolbox of strategies, exercises and ideas.

Another stepping-stone is to identify people with whom you could connect.

"WHO IS SAFE/SUPPORTIVE?"

1. In your notebook or journal, make a list of as many people you can think of.

2. For each person make a list of reasons why you do trust him or her *and* a list of why you don't trust him or her.

3. Rewrite your list including only those you can trust.

4. For each person identify how you want to contact him or her.

5. Schedule a date/time by which you want to reach out to anyone on your list.

6. Reach out.

Review your list of safe people. If you feel comfortable enough think of ways to meet up in person.

"WHERE COULD WE GO?
WHAT COULD WE DO?"

1. Grab a coffee at a coffee shop or bookstore.

2. Go to the movies.

3. Go to breakfast/lunch/ dinner.

4. Go to a play, musical, sporting event.

5. Don't forget to leave room in your notebook or journal to add ideas.

Keep in mind that the initial goal is to just be with other people. You don't have to explain your depression to anyone. When we feel depressed and begin to isolate, the depression is telling us, *Stay away from others. Don't talk to anyone. They don't understand anyway.* It's important to remember your values and what you believe is important. Our feeling of depression is telling us we don't want to be with others, but our value and what we really want oftentimes is to be with others. We are social creatures and need others. In order to achieve this value we need to take one step at a time. Before we can have deep conversations with people about how we are doing (if that is even a goal) we need to first just get together with people. No need for deep conversations about personal or intimate struggles right off the bat. One step at a time is the goal. The more you are with the safe people in your life the safer you will feel. The more safe you feel the more you will want to be with others and the less you will isolate yourself.

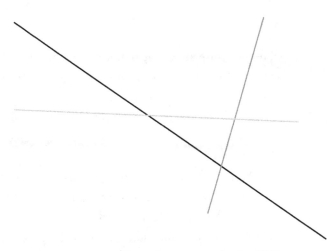

LOSS OF INTEREST & LACK OF ENERGY:
"I DON'T FEEL LIKE DOING ANYTHING."

Joan is a twenty-four year-old female nursing assistant. She lives with her boyfriend. She recently went to her primary care physician expressing concerns about having little or no energy. Joan used to look forward to working and now finds it hard to get out of bed. She sleeps whenever she can. In the last four weeks, Joan has called out of work three times. When her boyfriend Joe asks her to go out, Joan more often than not says, "Not today. Maybe some other time."

Mark is twenty and just completed his second year of college. He struggled to make it through the semester.

He's not sure about his major and is thinking about taking next semester off to figure things out. It has been a month since arriving back home and most days are filled with TV, video games, sleeping, or eating. Mark states, "Nothing I do feels good, and I no longer like anything I used to do."

Ann is forty, divorced and raising two teenagers. She works full-time as a bank manager. For the past six months, Ann has felt tired and overwhelmed. It takes all she has to work and take care of the house. She is not interested in dating "*at all.*" She feels lucky that her kids are fairly good and give her little trouble. She has two sisters who call all the time. Ann also has had a close friend, Cheryl, since grade school. She and Cheryl talk weekly but have not gone out together in six months. Ann thinks that life is just too much to handle and that everything she has to do is a chore. Ann loves her bed.

When we lose interest in activities we tend to also lose energy. The more we don't do things the more we don't want to do anything. The more we think about how tired we feel, the more tired we will be.

Remember the relationship between thoughts, behaviors, and feelings? They all interact and affect each other. When you are depressed, you often feel zapped of your energy supply. As a result, you tend to do less and less. However, imagine that activities are like gasoline for your car. When your car runs out of gas you need to fill up. When you are depressed and your tank is low on energy, how do you fill up?

"FILL 'ER UP"

1. In your journal or notebook make a list of things you do or used to like doing.

   a. Exercising, walking, etc.

   b. Going to a movie with a friend

   c. Work in the garden, pull weeds

   d. Play a video game or game on the computer

2. Recall a time you did two or three of the things on your list. Be as vividly descriptive as possible.

3. Imagine doing one of the things you listed.

4. Imagine feeling good about and energized by it. What would you be saying to yourself in order to feel energized and refueled?

   a. I loved pulling the weeds out of the garden. It relieved a lot of tension. As I pulled some weeds out I wanted to pull more and more out. I really worked up a sweat. The garden looked great when I was done. I felt good about what I accomplished. My family really liked how the garden looked. They said I did a great job. That felt good to hear. Each time I pass the garden I felt good.

b. Your turn. Write what you could say. Remember the goal is to feel energized. What can you say in order to reach that goal?

c. Pick one of the things from your list and go do it now!

5. After you are done, write, "Why I feel good." Don't write how you felt. You are to plan and predict that you *will* feel good.

Sometimes we cannot do things right now. Therefore, we need to plan or schedule them.

Use the following chart to plan an activity or two in the next week. You can break this down into one day or even one hour. In other words, you don't have to fill in an entire week of a calendar with an activity to do every hour on the hour. Pick one or two activities you will do this coming week and write them down. (The sooner you do one the sooner you will start to feel better.)

SCHEDULE IT, DO IT

In the next week, pick one or two days to schedule a time when you will do at least two of the things on your list.

Sunday:_____

Monday:_____

Tuesday: _____

Wednesday: Take a walk around the block._____

Thursday:_____

Friday:_____

Saturday: Go to the movies._____

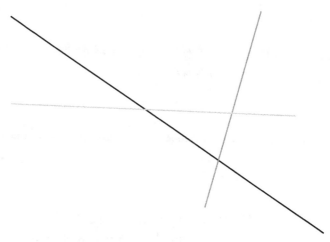

FEELING WORTHLESS/ GUILTY:

"WHO CARES ABOUT ME? I'M JUST A MESS UP."

Liz is the youngest of three girls. She is divorced and a single mom of two children, ages ten and seven. Her older sisters are "happily married" and each have two "great kids." Their husbands are wonderful, hard-working, and faithful men. Liz works as a nursing assistant in an elder care center. Liz often questions her past decisions regarding her life. She often feels alone and like she doesn't matter. Some of the thoughts Liz listens to every day in her head include:

I never should have married that loser.

I'm not fit to be a mom.

I should have finished my degree.

I have nothing to contribute (offer anyone).

Things just don't work out for me.

My life is a waste. No wonder I have no one in my life.

Steven is a junior in college. He gets Bs and sometimes Cs. He only has a few friends, but no one really close to him. He works part time in the resident hall. Most days involve going to classes, trying to study or complete assignments, working, and sleeping. He often feels like his parents are wasting their money sending him to college. He doubts whether he will ever "make anything of himself." The thoughts that typically take up space in his head include:

I'm not going to be anybody once I graduate. I'm nobody now.

If someone cared, I'd have friends.

My parents just feel sorry for me.

I'm such a disappointment.

Joan is a forty-eight-year-old married woman. Her daughter is a senior in high school, and her son is a sophomore in college. She lives with her husband who is an attorney. Joan works part time at a nursery because she loves plants. From the outside, Joan appears to have it all. On the inside, Joan struggles every day with depression. Joan was first diagnosed with depression when she was sixteen. She sees a therapist weekly and a psychiatrist every month for medication. She has been psychiatrically hospitalized three different times in the past ten years. Joan feels worthless as a person and believes she is a burden to her family.

Some of the thoughts that Joan has playing in her head include:

I am worthless.

I have no talent or abilities.

My family deserves better.

Feeling worthless or guilty can easily drain you of energy. It can delay or prevent motivation. When we don't feel worthy or valued, it's easy to put ourselves down. If you feel worthless or guilty, you are likely to dismiss compliments or positive aspects of your life. As with most symptoms of depression, feeling worthless or guilty is reinforced by our self-talk. Our life circumstances may also reinforce such feelings, but remember what you can control and what you cannot control.

"THINGS I DO"

One way to decrease feeling worthless is by looking for your value. Jot down all you do in a day. This can include things like:

- Make lunches for the kids

- Help a friend with homework or an assignment

- Lend a friend or neighbor something

- Drive the kids to an activity

- Attend classes

- Study and do my work

- Make dinner

- Do laundry

- Pay bills

- Go to work

- Cut the lawn

- Water the plants

- Feed the dog

I'm sure you do some of these activities and many, many more. Use your journal or notebook to keep track. You will soon see all that you do.

Now you might say:

- "Nobody appreciates what I do."

- "I have to do those things. It's just expected."

- "The things I do, anyone can do."

- "What I do is not significant."

These messages are thinking errors. They minimize or dismiss you and what you do. This is how you devalue yourself and make yourself feel worthless. This is that negative, reinforced cycle, which fuels depression and keeps you down. Instead of minimizing what you do try the opposite. Acknowledge each activity and add positive comments to it as in the exercise below. Read over the examples below and then try making up some yourself.

WORTHLESS TO WORTHY!

"Making lunches or driving the kids places is important. It is one of the many ways I show my love for my kids."

"When I help someone (at work or home) I am being thoughtful. Being thoughtful is a worthy characteristic. I am good at helping others."

"Volunteering or working makes a difference; therefore, I make a difference."

"Attending college is a great opportunity for me and I deserve it."

Use your list of "Things I do" and add positive comments for each one. Read over your list including the positive comments every day for the next few weeks. Try adding to the list as often as you can.

If it is hard to acknowledge yourself and find value in what you do, try asking those that are close to you what they value about you. There are many ways to ask this question. Instead of value you can substitute phrases like:

"What do you like about me?"

"What things do I do that you like?"

"What's good about me?"

Remember to accept the positives you hear and avoid dismissing or minimizing the comments.

If you would rather be less personal try asking others about the activities you do from your "Things I Do" list.

Ask things like:

> "Do you think that making lunches for my kids is nice to do?"
>
> "Is going to college good or important?"
>
> "Is helping others a worthy endeavor?"

In reading these questions to yourself, you might feel like, *This is silly. Of course the answers are yes.* This is because we often tend to work from the perspective of a double standard: "If someone else is doing it, then it's a worthy activity, and they're a valued person. If I do it, it's no big deal. I should be doing it."

We also tend to stay in our heads. It makes perfect sense in there! It's only when we say it out loud or challenge such thinking that we realize that our thinking might be a little flawed.

Sometimes when we don't feel worthy or a sense of value we also feel a sense of guilt. When it comes to managing or overcoming feeling guilty it is important to ask yourself several questions.

"Should I feel guilty?"

"Did I do something wrong?"

"Was it malicious?"

If the answer is no we need to explain to ourselves why we don't need to feel guilty. If we did do something wrong and it was not intentionally malicious, then ask yourself, *Is it okay to not be perfect and, therefore, make mistakes?* Many times we set an unreachable bar for ourselves—perfection! This is clearly unrealistic, yet we still expect it of ourselves. This can be a setup for failure and a way for us to continue the cycle of beating ourselves up. Keep in mind that habit of having a double standard: *It's okay for others to make mistakes, but I have to be perfect!*

This leads to another question to ask yourself, *If I switched places with someone else, would I forgive them?* Chances are the answer would be yes. We need to give ourselves a break once and a while. Forgiveness is a gift you give yourself and can be very freeing. It takes a lot of energy to hold on to anger or resentment. No one has to tell you that the more you put yourself down and hold yourself to such an unrealistic expectation the worse you feel.

Another way to look at guilt is that sometimes it is healthy. Guilt helps us to know the difference between right and wrong. It helps us to try and do what is right. But how long should you feel guilty? The longer we beat ourselves up and don't forgive ourselves, the longer we will feel bad. When we feel guilty long enough and consistently, we often feel depressed. This habit, like many others, becomes automatic after a while. We need to break the habit and break the cycle. One way to do this is to make a list of whatever you feel guilty about and blame yourself for. Then write yourself a letter of forgiveness.

I FORGIVE ME LETTER

The idea of forgiving ourselves sounds easy and makes sense. Doing it is another story. If this is true for you, start by writing the letter addressed to someone you care about. Pretend you are forgiving this friend. Afterward go back and replace their name with your name. Read it. Then read it again a few times more until you develop a level of comfort. During the process notice the negative, minimizing comments you might make such as: *This is dumb; I don't deserve forgiveness; I can't let this go; this won't work.* These negative defeating comments keep you depressed. They keep the negative cycle going. You don't want to feel depressed anymore. It feels awful. You can do this! You deserve to feel better. The more you say the positive, the more you will learn to believe them about yourself.

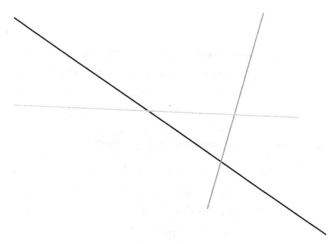

HOPELESS/SUICIDAL:
"NOTHING WILL EVER CHANGE. I SHOULD JUST END IT."

Natalie is a nineteen-year-old college freshman. She is struggling to get through her first semester. She has been partying more than attending classes or studying. She's trying desperately to "pull it together" but has no faith in her ability to do it. Her parents and family won't understand. Her friends just like her when she's partying. Natalie is thinking:

> *What's the point?*
>
> *I can't change.*
>
> *I'll always be a screw up.*
>
> *I can't do this anymore.*

Claire is forty years old. She is married with a fifteen-year-old daughter. Her husband works "a lot." She quit work to raise her daughter and never went back. Now she fills her day gardening, cooking, and avoiding others. Claire has ongoing memories of child abuse that just won't go away. She will drink or take her "meds," sometimes both, to sleep. She sleeps whenever she can. When she's awake, Claire is often thinking about hurting herself and/or ending it all. Claire struggles daily with the following types of thoughts:

> *I can't go on another five minutes.*
>
> *I'll never be okay.*
>
> *Nobody gets it anyway, why should I stick around?*
>
> *They'll all be better off without me.*

Barry is about to turn fifty. He is facing divorce for the second time, bankruptcy, and losing his home. He works to escape being alone but can't stand what he does. Nighttime is the worst. He can't sleep because he worries constantly. He's fighting his weight and diabetes numbers. The kids are barely talking to him. They blame him for the family break-up. Barry struggles with the following types of thoughts:

> *Why doesn't anything work out for me?*
>
> *I've screwed up one too many times.*
>
> *I'll never learn.*
>
> *They need to forgive me.*
>
> *The hell with it, my life sucks, and it'll never get better.*

Jason is a thirty-two year old physical therapist. Up until age thirty, he was living with his mother. For the past two years, he really enjoyed his job and living on his own. That changed a month ago when he got a new boss. Jason feels his boss doesn't like him. His boss frequently tells Jason what he is doing wrong. Jason has started missing work in the last two weeks and is feeling like things are not going to get any better. Most days, Jason is focusing on the following types of thoughts:

I'm never going to enjoy my job again.

I won't be able to get another job because my boss will give me a terrible reference.

My life is over.

I can't do this anymore.

As you can see from the previous stories and scenarios, life situations can become so unbearable that sometimes depressive thoughts can lead to feeling hopeless and wanting to end life. Sometimes, perhaps most times, we really just want the pain or the problem to stop and go away. When we feel hopeless, we are thinking and starting to believe that there is no way life will change or get better. Sometimes you may feel that you have tried everything but nothing has changed the situation. Unfortunately, some situations are not changeable.

If someone has a chronic illness, a permanent disability, or experiences a loss, these situations can't be "fixed." If someone has been abused in some way, nothing can change that. Such realities can be extremely difficult to accept or live with. The key here is to recognize that such life circumstances are extremely difficult to live with or accept; yet it is possible to live with and accept them.

Let's break down this idea or belief that "we can't live with such situations." What do we require to live? Essentially, in order to live we need air, water, food, and shelter. You could also argue that we need clothing, maybe some people around us since we are social beings. After reading these last two lines you might be saying, "That's not what I mean by living." Perhaps what you mean is that you can't stand living with such memories of the abuse. Or you can't stand living with such limitations from your chronic illness or disability. Or you can't stand living without your husband (or whoever has passed away). In other words, living under such circumstances is unbelievably difficult and makes a person question what's the point. If things can't change, then—then what? How do you answer this question? This is the crux of the issue. When we become hopeless or suicidal we answer this question by saying, "If things can't change then life is hopeless, and I might as well give up. I can't do it. I can't go on." What if we change that perception or thought to, *Moving on is so painfully hard to do?*

This means *you can* move on *and* it is going to be very difficult. A question you might want to address when feeling this way is, "What's the point? Why should I move on or try anymore?" Read over the following list of what people just like you came up with. See if you can identify with any.

I want to move on because:

- I really don't want to feel this bad anymore.

- I want to finally get a break.

- My spouse loves me.

- My kids love me.

- I love my dog and don't want him to be alone.

- I don't want to die.

- Add as many other reasons for why you want to move on as you can in your journal.

While reading these reasons you were probably thinking, *Yeah that's true, but it's too hard* or *I can't*. There's that negative voice again. It's really difficult to get away from it. So don't. That's right. Don't try to stop thinking negatively. It doesn't work.

The reason it doesn't work is because the more you try to resist something the more it will persist.

What you resist will persist! Don't believe it? Try to not think of the color red. Go ahead. See? You were thinking of it weren't you? In trying not to think of something you actually are paying attention to it. The more you attend to something the more you think about it and thus the cycle begins!

Instead of trying not to think negatively, try to think positively or at least about something else other than that negative voice.

Use your senses to help. Try the following exercise.

USING OUR SENSES

When you are stuck in a negative thought try tuning into your senses.

What do you hear?

What do you smell?

What do you see?

What can you feel? (Use your hands, feet if you are standing, legs and butt if you are sitting).

What can you taste?

Try to describe your answers in as much vivid detail as possible. Read the following as an example: I hear the birds chirping and some birds flying by. I hear my neighbor's air conditioner running. I hear three kids playing ball in their back yard. They are yelling about the game they are playing. I feel the light breeze of the wind. I feel the cushion I am sitting on. It is firm but soft and comfortable. I feel my sandals as I grip my toes.

I see the flowers in my garden. There are yellow, purple, and pink ones. I see my neighbor's backyard and his deck with a loveseat and two chairs. There's a small table and a gas grill. The loveseat has some pillows on it. They are brown and tan. On the railing are three ceramic frogs.

Now you use your senses and describe with even more detail what you hear, see, feel, smell, and taste.

By focusing on your senses you are leaving the negative voice. I bet you will agree that thinking about what you hear, see, feel, smell, and taste is a lot better than listening to the nagging, annoying negative voice.

By creating this other focus you develop distance from the negative thoughts. This distraction can allow you to move away from feeling negative or feeling so hopeless. That's the goal right?

Now you might be thinking, *Okay. I can do that, but it won't last!* There's that, "Yes, but ..." Anytime you dismiss or minimize something you do you are typically falling into the, "Yes, but ..." trap. Try to notice such thoughts and write them down on the left side of a piece of paper. Divide the page, and on the right side rewrite the statement using, "Yes, and ..." Use the chart below as a start.

Table 7.A Yes, ~~but~~ And...

Yes, but	Yes, and
Yes, I can try focusing on my senses but it won't last.	Yes, I can use my senses and it helps to focus on better things than my negative thoughts.
Yes, I can think of those that care about me, but I am tired of trying. Life is too hard.	Yes I can think of those who care about me and I can try to care about myself too. If I did, I would feel better about me.
Yes, people care but I can't live for others the memories of the abuse are too much.	Yes other people care about me and in time I can learn to care for me too. The memories of the abuse are there and so are other memories – positive ones, memories of happy things that have happened.

Another reason some people feel hopeless is because they have been depressed for a long time. Keep in mind the depression doesn't stay at the same level of intensity all the time. You might think it does, but it really doesn't. We can be depressed for weeks, months, and even years, and during that time we can also not be depressed. In other words, sometimes depression is a recurrent or chronic condition. Therefore, one can say, "I've been depressed since I was a teenager." However, that incorrectly implies that you have been depressed all day every day for years. This is not true. Although you may not realize it, you have had moments of not being depressed. Have you ever watched a show and laughed? Have you ever talked with someone and smiled? The point is that when we feel depressed we focus on things that reinforce feeling that way. If you were to keep track of your level of depression, you would see that this fluctuates. The more you notice the times you are not as depressed—or, might we dare say, good—the more you will develop a sense of hope.

TRACKING MY LEVEL

You can check this out throughout the day such as at breakfast, lunch, dinner, and before going to sleep. You can use a scale of zero to ten or zero to one hundred. You can also use mild, moderate, or severe. Another option is to rate yourself once a day. You could use a calendar to do this. If your calendar has blocks for each day like on a wall calendar you could color each block to signify your level of feeling depressed or hopelessness. Black could indicate total hopelessness and despair. Yellow could indicate feeling great and not feeling hopeless or depressed at all. You could also track this weekly by using the depression screening in the appendix. Try to track your level over the next month. After the month, put the results into a chart, and you will see how your depression level fluctuates.

Once you are able to see the evidence that your depression level fluctuates you can use that to challenge your belief that things are hopeless. If they were hopeless, then things would not change. If things can change or improve at times, then things can't be hopeless. You can also look at the times when your depression level is better and try to identify what was different during those times. Who were you with? What were you doing? Most importantly, what were you thinking during that time? Get out your journal and use the following exercise to figure this out.

WHAT'S DIFFERENT WHEN I AM FEELING OKAY AND WHEN I AM FEELING DEPRESSED?

When I am Feeling Okay:

This is what I tend to think about...

_____

_____

_____

This is what I tend to be doing…

_____

_____

_____

This is whom I tend to be with…

_____

_____

When I am Feeling Depressed:
This is what I tend to think about…

_____

_____

_____

This is what I tend to be doing…

_____

_____

_____

This is whom I tend to be with…

_____

_____

The more you are able to recognize and notice what you are doing, thinking, and who you are with when you are depressed, the more control you develop in being able to change it. Remember in order to change something you need to know when you are doing it. The first step to change is awareness. If you are like most of us you will want this change to occur immediately! However, that is not reality. Chances are you will not be aware of your thoughts, behaviors, and whom you are with at any given time because it's not something you typically tune into. When we are depressed, and especially if we have been depressed for sometime, our thoughts, actions, and whom we tend to be around is pretty automatic. This will take time and practice.

CHECK-IN

One way to create this new habit is to schedule times to check in with yourself. So perhaps in the morning, afternoon, and evening you can take two minutes and journal what you are thinking about, what you are doing, and who you are around. Then rate your feeling of depression. You might want to set a timer or alarm on your watch or cell phone as a reminder. This habit will not come easily, so keep at it. Experts say that it takes thirty days to create a new habit!!

Earlier I said that the first step to change involves awareness. Think of the typical problem solving steps. There are usually five steps.

Step 1: Identifying the problem.

Step 2: Brainstorming options of what you can do.

Step 3: Picking an option from your list.

Step 4: Trying the option that you picked.

Step 5: Evaluating the degree that the option you tried was effective.

If you determine that an option is not that effective you must repeat steps two through five.

When you integrate cognitive therapy into the problem solving steps it looks like the following:

Step 1: Identify the problem (e.g. depression). ***

Step 2: Become aware of the problem (e.g. what are you thinking, doing, and who are you around when you are depressed).

Step 3: Decide what you want (e.g. How or what do I want to be thinking? What do I want to be doing? Whom do I want to be around?).

Note: Try not to focus on "I don't feel like doing anything." Instead focus on what you want. "I want to feel less depressed," "I want to not feel depressed." Then what do you need to be thinking and doing?

Step 4: Practice what you want (e.g. thinking positively, doing something for you, being with someone).

Step 5: Evaluate what you did (e.g. Was thinking positively, doing something for you, and being with someone is better than not doing any of those things?)

The more you practice thinking and acting in a non-depressed way, the more you will overcome or manage the depression.

ONE NOTCH UP ON THE CONTINUUM

At this point you might be thinking, *If I could think more positively and do more things for myself or stop isolating I wouldn't feel so hopeless—but I can't!* There's that, "Yes, but..." again. Try looking at this as one step at a time. Remember the continuum concept. The long-term goal might be to get to the other end and feel total joy and happiness. The immediate goal is to move one step up the continuum. Recognize and become aware of where you are on the continuum right now. What would you be doing, and thinking if you moved up the continuum just one notch?

For example, Jackie has not left the house in over a week. One notch up would be stepping out onto the porch for a little while.

John just comes home from work, eats dinner, and goes right to bed with minimal conversation with his family. One notch up might be for John to help clean up after dinner.

Mary gets the kids off to school and goes right back to bed every day for two to three hours. One notch up might be for Mary to delay going back to bed. Instead of going right back to bed after the kids get on the bus, Mary could read for a little while or make a grocery list, or call a friend.

If you take a bunch of small steps you can soon realize that you've come a long way.

Sometimes you find that the "small" step you tried was actually too big. In order to increase your level of success, make sure that the steps you decide to try are realistic and achievable. No sense in setting yourself up to fail. Anytime you discover that the step you planned to try wasn't achievable, break it down into smaller steps.

BREAK IT DOWN

Art Freeman in his book *Woulda, Coulda, Shoulda: Overcoming Regrets, Mistakes and Missed Opportunities* describes how making pasta can involve as many as twenty-one steps. Think about it. How many steps would it take you to make and serve pasta? Almost any task you set out to do can be broken down into steps. Therefore, the key is to break down the task into steps that you *can* do. Once you achieve one step you've just proven that things aren't hopeless!

ONE DAY AT A TIME

Another idea to combat hopelessness is to focus on one day at a time. People in AA have used this slogan for years—very effectively I might add. Oftentimes in feeling hopeless we see the future as very bleak. Focusing on one day at a time decreases the sense of being overwhelmed by the idea that the rest of your life will be awful. One day at a time follows the "break things down into smaller steps" idea. Life is much more manageable when you take it one day at a time.

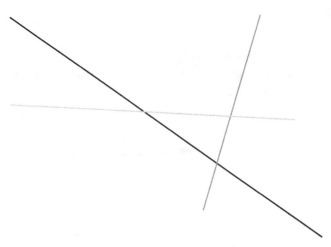

TOO MUCH OR TOO LITTLE EATING/SLEEPING:

"I'M NOT TAKING CARE OF ME."

Amanda is a thirty-three-year-old mother of three children. She has been married for seven years. In the past month Amanda has been having trouble getting to sleep three or four nights a week. She feels tired, but when she gets in bed she just can't fall asleep. It takes her hours to finally fall asleep.

Mike is twenty-six and lives with his girlfriend of over a year. Mike has been late to work several times in the past few weeks because he is unable to get up on time. He feels tired "all the time." On days off, Mike takes naps for one to two hours and is still tired at night.

Jeff is twenty-one and lives with his parents and two younger brothers. Jeff has gained fifteen pounds in the past two months. He is eating "all the time" especially at night after everyone has gone to bed. Jeff describes worrying about his future and feeling like a failure. He is recovering from drug and alcohol abuse and has six months clean. He often avoids social settings because he is afraid of not knowing what to say. Drugs and alcohol used to act as a social lubricant. Now that he is clean, Jeff has been having an increase in anxiety. Eating helps.

Lisa is forty-five and was recently discharged from an inpatient psychiatric facility. She has been depressed "all her life." Lisa struggles to eat consistently. She isn't always sure if she deserves to eat. She also feels stronger and more in control when she doesn't eat. Lisa also struggles with self-image and believes she is so ugly—"Why take care of myself?"

Eating and sleeping are essential elements to one's overall mental and physical health. When feeling depressed eating and sleeping habits are often disrupted. Sometimes we can feel tired all the time and feel like we can never get enough sleep. Other times, sleep can seem like an unreachable goal. We just can't turn our minds off, and we just watch the clock hour after hour. Likewise our desire to eat can vary just as much. Some days you might have an appetite, and other days the idea of eating anything can be either repulsive or just not very appealing.

There can be numerous explanations for individuals struggling with depression and experiencing problems with sleeping and/or eating. Usually people struggling with depression will eat or not eat as a way to deal with their emotions. Emotional eating is a huge problem for many, many people. This is especially true with people struggling with depression and/or anxiety. There are numerous contributing factors. Sleeping problems are often affected by a person's energy level, activity level, sleeping habits, and the medications they are taking (substance use/abuse will also affect sleep). Over sleeping can be an intentional way to avoid and isolate or as a way of "dealing" with intense emotions. Stress is another contributing factor. When we are stressed the body releases a hormone known as cortisol. Cortisol is often referred to as the "stress hormone." When we are overly stressed we get an overload of cortisol. This overload of cortisol often creates cravings for salty foods and/or sweets, thus affecting our eating habits.

So what is a person to do? There are plenty of options and ideas.

EXERCISE

Exercise has multiple benefits. In addition to exercise helping you lose weight or stay fit, exercise can help boost your energy level. The exercise I'm referring to does not need to involve spending a bunch of money for a gym membership and spending an hour three days a week doing something you can't stand. Exercise can be simple and even enjoyable. Go for a walk either by yourself for some peace and quiet or with a friend or spouse to nurture a relationship. If you have a dog, taking a daily walk is part of being a responsible pet owner. If you don't "feel like" walking for you, do it for your dog. A brisk walk will help give you some energy. One reason for the increase in energy level is because light exercise can decrease tension and stress. Exercise can help decrease the levels of cortisol, the stress hormone, and increase the release of endorphins in your body, which makes us feel good. If you don't like walking and don't have a dog, try yoga. There are plenty of yoga DVDs available in stores or maybe even at some yard sales. You might be able to find one through your TV programming. Such light exercises do not over-stimulate the body. Therefore, doing yoga or taking a walk a couple of hours before going to sleep can actually relax you.

FOLLOW A BED TIME AND WAKE UP ROUTINE

By going to bed around the same time and waking up around the same time your body develops a habit, which in time can become automatic. If you have kids, you have probably noticed that by putting them to bed at a regular time and getting them up at a regular time kind of programs them. They still get up on weekends even when you want them to sleep in! In order to create a routine follow these steps: First, figure out a reasonable time to go to bed and when you should wake up. Second, plan a few different activities to do before bed to help relax you and prepare your body for sleep. With kids, parents will often read them a bedtime story. Well, that doesn't just work with kids. If you like to read get some books you have some interest in. If you don't like to read try some word puzzle books or Sudoku. Third, get in bed and close your eyes. Focus on your breathing and think about your body being very relaxed. If you are still awake after thirty or forty minutes try some of the ideas in step two again. Don't stay in bed. Get up and try something to relax your body and your mind.

Other ideas to prepare for sleep include:

- Plan to take a hot shower or on some nights maybe a bubble bath.

- Listen to some soothing music.

- Meditate or practice relaxation strategies like deep breathing or progressive muscle relaxation. These are great techniques, which segue smoothly into sleeping since they relax our body and clear our mind. (These are described in detail in the appendix section on "How to Relax.")

Sometimes our mind just won't shut off. One way to deal with this is by journaling. Journaling is a great way to clear our minds or process our thoughts and feelings about the day. It can help us prepare for the next day as well.

JOURNALING

Try writing down the concerns you have running through your mind. Perhaps you are worried about something. If so, write what you are worried about, and then write what you want to do about it. Remember to focus on you and what you have control over. Worries are often about things that have happened or that you think will happen. We can't change those things that have already happened. We can acknowledge what took place and how we feel and think. We can also think about what we will do to prevent that same thing from happening again. For things we are worried about happening in the future, we can develop a plan of action or prevention. By journaling what you are thinking about and a response to your worries we can sometimes ease our minds and slow things down enough to fall asleep.

You can also journal about what you are thankful for or appreciate. This can help create a positive spin or positive focus. Just take some time and identify two or three things that you appreciate about your life and that happened that day.

APPRECIATION JOURNAL

- It was sunny out today. It finally stopped raining.

- No one bothered me today.

- I didn't get any calls from telemarketers.

- I went for a walk with my dog, and we both enjoyed it. I love having a dog.

- My flowers started blooming today, and they look beautiful.

- Dinner was ready when I got home from work.

- I have air conditioning.

- My family ate what I made for dinner.

In your journal, rewrite this list. Over the next few days, weeks, and months try to write more things that you are thankful for or appreciate.

CLEAN

If you are like most people, there is a fair amount of clutter in your home. Having clutter can create stress, which can lead to trouble sleeping. By cleaning up and putting some things away you can feel more relaxed. Waking up to a cleaner house with less clutter can lead you to have a more restful sleep.

Some things to avoid before going to sleep include:

- Don't drink caffeine after 2:00 pm.

- Stop drinking fluids two hours or so before going to sleep to decrease the need to go to the bathroom during the night.

- Don't eat large amounts of food before going to bed. If you eat a snack, try eating small amounts of dairy foods or rich carbohydrate foods. This means a small snack, not a meal. These foods contain the sleep inducing substance called tryptophan.

- Avoid smoking a couple hours before going to sleep. Nicotine, like caffeine, is a stimulant.

- Don't engage in confrontational or emotionally intense conversations.

- Don't try to figure out your finances. This can increase worries and stress.

- Don't watch television shows or movies that are over-stimulating or emotionally charged.

Similar to sleeping problems, eating is also affected when we are feeling depressed. Many of the suggestions just offered for improving sleep can also be used for improving eating patterns. Journaling is a good way to express what you are feeling instead of using food as a way to find comfort or to punish ourselves. If you are using food to satisfy an emotional void, you must first become aware of doing this. Journaling what you are thinking about and feeling before you eat can help increase your awareness. You might also identify a pattern to your eating habits and certain triggers. For example you might be eating ice cream whenever you are feeling sad or lonely. You might avoid eating whenever you feel guilty or bad. This emotional eating is very powerful, and recognizing how your emotional responses are influencing your decision about whether to eat or not or what you choose to eat is the first step to correcting this problem.

Keep in mind the following differences between emotional eating and hunger.

1. Emotional hunger comes on suddenly and feels like it needs to be satisfied right then, whereas physical hunger occurs in a more gradual process, and you can wait to eat.

2. When you are eating to fill an emotional void you typically crave a specific food such as pizza or ice cream and only that food will meet your need. When you eat because you are hungry, your food options aren't so limited.

3. When you are eating in response to emotions, you're more likely to keep eating even after you are full. When you're eating because you're hungry, you're more likely to stop when you're full.

4. After eating to fill an emotional void you will feel guilty and even angry. This is not the case when you eat because you are hungry.

Sometimes the problem isn't always overeating or emotional eating but the opposite. Sometimes depression influences us to have no appetite. This can be due to not feeling worthy or as a self-inflicted punishment or because you just don't care anymore. Obviously you need to address the emotions related to you not wanting to eat and challenge the thinking process related to feeling that way. You can use many of the strategies already discussed previously in the book. Additionally, you can start to plan to eat. Remember it's important to identify the value and what you believe is important. The double standard is often at play here. You wouldn't be telling a friend or loved one, "Not eating is okay." Also remember the continuum concept. If you are eating one meal a day, one notch up the continuum might be one meal and a snack. Keep in mind to take one step at a time and focus on today.

EAT WITH A SUPPORT PERSON

Remember the individuals you identified as safe and supportive. Ask one of these support people to lunch or to grab coffee/tea and a bagel.

COOK

Sometimes by cooking we want to taste what we make. This could wet your appetite. The cooking doesn't have to be a nine-course meal. Perhaps you just make soup. Maybe you bake a pie. Make it for someone else, and they will probably want you to join them.

PICK FOODS YOU LIKE

Whether you go food shopping or someone else does it for you, pick food you like and have eaten before. This is similar to trying activities that you used to like doing. You are more likely to eat things you like than those you can't stand!

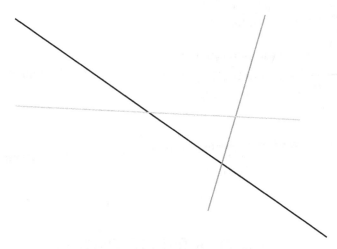

ADDITIONAL STRATEGIES & SUGGESTIONS:
"WHAT ELSE CAN I DO?"

GET A FULL PHYSICAL

There are many medical conditions that can cause the various symptoms associated with depression. Therefore, it is important to rule out any physical condition. Get a full physical to rule out any medical conditions that could be contributing to your symptoms.

SUSPEND JUDGMENT

You may consider your situation as hopeless or at least next to impossible. If so, you have nothing to lose by trying the exercises and suggestions throughout this book. Keep an open mind for now and try thinking in terms of the following:

What if I could change how I'm feeling?

What if I could develop more control over my thinking patterns?

What if I started to focus on the positives in my life?

HOW MUCH DOES IT COST?

If you are having trouble getting motivated to change your behavior and challenge your thinking patterns, perhaps you should evaluate the costs and rewards to maintaining your current situation.

If I don't change:

- I will continue to have predominantly negative thoughts about my situation, my future, and myself.

- I will continue to live mostly alone with little or no rewarding interactions with others.

- I will spend hundreds or thousands of dollars every year in co-pays for therapy, medication appointments and medicines.

- I will continue to have little or no energy and feel tired most of the time.

- I will struggle to get through each day at home.

- I will continue to struggle each day or each week at work (perhaps I will not be able to work anymore).

- I will continue to feel bad, hopeless, and/or helpless.

- My relationships with loved ones will continue to be strained.

Take some time to rewrite this list in your journal or notebook and leave space to add other costs to you not changing your situation.

If I were to change, the rewards or benefits would include:

- I would feel better and less overwhelmed about my situation, my future, and me.

- I would smile and laugh more.

- I would enjoy my relationships more.

- I could concentrate more and be able to finish reading a book.

- I could sleep more restfully.

- I'd eat better and feel healthier.

- I would look forward to waking up.

- I'd have goals.

- I would enjoy my interests and hobbies again.

- I'd have friends and better relationships with my loved ones and support system.

- I might not have to take as many medications.

- I would not spend as much money on medications and doctor appointments.

- I would have less doctor appointments to make and go to.

- I could get back to work.

- I could perform better at work.

- I could do better in school.

- I could finish my degree.

- I would feel better.

- I would be more in charge of how I feel and for how long I feel that way.

Get your journal back out and list some other benefits or rewards to you changing, which will in turn change your situation.

MAKE REMINDERS OF WHAT HELPS

As you read through the book take note of which strategies and suggestions work best for you. Which ones do you like the most? You can record these in a journal and title it "Things that Help." You could write things down on sticky notes or post cards and keep them in your purse, car, or at your desk. Use your computer, and put some ideas on your screen saver or background. If you actively keep a calendar on your computer or in your phone, you can program reminders with alarms.

LOOK FOR THE POSITIVE EVERY DAY: MY POSITIVE JOURNAL

When we are feeling depressed, it is much easier to find the negative. Try doing the opposite instead. Look for and record things that were positive about each day. In your positive journal write down ten things that were positive about your day. Be sure to think of at least three or more different things than the previous day.

WHAT ARE MY RED FLAGS TO BEING DEPRESSED?

As you might have guessed, the red flags are primarily the symptoms of depression described in chapters 3 through 8. Oftentimes, we don't notice these symptoms until they reach the moderate or severe level. Try reviewing the exercises "Tracking My Level" and "What's Different When I Am Feeling Okay and When I Am Feeling Depressed?" in chapter 7. Use these to identify the red flags or warning signals to your level of depression returning or getting worse. You can also review the scenarios described in the beginning of each chapter. These scenarios can help you put into words what depression feels like.

In addition to the symptoms of depression, red flags can also include various stressors, which we may or may not be able to predict or prevent. However, if you know that you are prone to stress or have a hard time dealing effectively with stress try writing down typical stressors.

TYPICAL STRESSORS

- Conflict with someone
- Loss or rejection (This can be perceived/ anticipated or actual loss or rejection experience.)
- Financial stress
- Work pressure
- School pressure
- Deadlines and due dates
- Having to make an uncomfortable decision
- Having to do something that is anxiety provoking
- Anniversary (birthday, holiday, etc.) of a loss
- Family gathering
- Health concerns
- Other (In your journal try listing a few stressors pertinent to you)

TOP FIVE RED FLAGS

Now review the list of red flags and identify the top five that affect you the most. Rewrite the top five, and keep this as a separate list. Try to review this top-five list on a weekly basis. Remember, the more in tune we are, the better we can catch the depression early and intervene. The longer we go, the more severe the symptoms become and the greater the challenge is to pull ourselves out of the dark hole.

NAME THE NEGATIVE AND CREATE DISTANCE

Once you have identified the red flags, then you have to notice when you are experiencing them. This can be a slippery slope if you are prone to beating yourself up. If you notice you are falling into that black hole, one way to go even deeper is by putting yourself down with self-blaming comments and thoughts of hopelessness. Instead of personalizing things, try creating some distance between the negative thought and you. If you start to blame yourself for failing or not being good enough, try reframing the situation and tell yourself, *There's that critic.* This way the voice is negative *not you.* You can also say things like, *There's that depression, trying to rear its ugly head.*

CHANGE THE SCENERY

Part of being depressed often involves isolating and avoiding interactions with others. We stop doing things that re-energize us. Sometimes we find staying in our home or even our room feels safer. Unfortunately, this also reinforces the depression. Trying a change of scenery can help break the pattern of isolating and avoiding. Keep in mind the concepts of breaking things down into small steps and the continuum. What would one step up the continuum look like? Perhaps this involves sitting out on the balcony or porch. Perhaps going for a walk around the block. Perhaps you could go to a coffee shop and read a book. Whatever you have been doing, try doing something different. Sometimes by being in a new setting we can create a new feeling.

DEVELOP COGNITIVE FLEXIBILITY

In order to gain a greater sense of control over your moods, practice changing your mood by changing your thoughts. Pick a feeling you want to have, and identify the thoughts you would need to reinforce that feeling. Now rehearse those thoughts and concentrate on the feeling you picked. After three to five minutes pick a second feeling. Identify the thoughts you would need to reinforce that feeling. Stay with the second feeling for a few minutes and either switch back to the first feeling or identify a third feeling to experience. The more you learn how to pick the feeling you want and realize how you can feel, the stronger you will feel over the depression. To optimize this experience, try pairing the thoughts with a behavior that would match the feeling you picked. By thinking and doing things that reinforce a feeling, the stronger you will experience that feeling. Just thinking happy thoughts usually isn't enough. If we think positively and do something that's good for us, we are more likely to experience positive feelings.

CHANGE THE "I SHOULD ... "

If you struggle with being a perfectionist or trying to live up to someone else's standards you probably have a lot of "I should have's" in your head. One way to alter this unrealistic thought pattern is to substitute the "I should have" with "I'd prefer" or "It would be better if..." This minor adjustment gives you a break. It points out what you want or wish without imposing an unrealistic expectation or standard. Try writing out a list of "I should have" statements on the left side of the page, and on the right side substitute "I should have" with "I'd prefer."

"I SHOULD HAVE ... "	"I'D PREFER ... " OR "IT WOULD BE BETTER IF ... "
I should have finished my degree.	It would be better if I finish my degree.
I should have taken that other job.	I would prefer a different job.
I should have been nicer.	I would prefer to be nicer.
I should have known how to do this.	It would be better if I knew how to do this.

Try to add some of your own "I should have" statements and practice substituting "I'd prefer" or "It would be better if..." It's okay to ask for help with this exercise!

COMMON MEDICATIONS USED TO TREAT DEPRESSION

In addition to counseling or "talk therapy," medications are often used as a treatment for depression. There are numerous types of medications available. This is good news and bad news. The good news is that if one medication or one combination of medications do not work, there are many more to try. The bad news is that you may have to try a lot of medications and combinations of medications before learning which works best for you.

It is important to remember that medications are designed to change certain brain chemicals called neurotransmitters. Medications can help you produce more of or block the production of these neurotransmitters. By changing the amount of certain neurotransmitters in the brain, you will have a change in your emotions. Unfortunately, changes in the brain chemicals can also cause various side effects. Some are positive such as slowing down racing thoughts and helping you to have better concentration. Others are negative such as decreasing your sex drive or increasing appetite. Before taking any medication, be sure to have a thorough evaluation by a trained professional, such as a psychiatrist. Even though a large percentage of medications for depression are prescribed by family doctors and primary care physicians it is best to be evaluated by a professional trained specifically in the ability to diagnosis and treat depression.

The primary depression medications can be grouped into the various categories listed below.

Monoamine oxidase inhibitors (MAOIs) are a category of medications that were used early on in the treatment of depression. These medications are usually effective in people who do not respond to other treatments for depression. They are also effective for other mental illnesses. Substances in certain foods like cheese, beverages like wine, and medications can interact with an MAOI, so these people taking this medication must adhere to strict dietary restrictions. (Be sure to check with your doctor for a complete list of which foods to avoid.) For this reason these antidepressants also aren't usually the first drugs used.

The following include the more common MAOIs prescribed.

Table 10.A MAOI Medications

Brand Name	Generic name	Dose Range up to Maximum Daily Dose
Marplan	Isocarboxazid	10mg up to 60mg
Nardil	Phenelzine	15mg up to 90mg
Parnate	Tranylcypromine	10mg up to 60mg

Norepinephrine dopamine reuptake inhibitors are another group of medications that work to change the level of norepinephrine and dopamine available in the brain. The following is a list of the more common norepinephrine dopamine reuptake inhibitors prescribed.

Table 10.B Norepinephrine Dopamine Reuptake Inhibitor Medication

Brand Name	Generic Name	Dose Range up to Maximum Daily Dose
Wellbutrin	Bupropion	75mg, and 100mg up to 450mg
Wellbutrin SR	Bupropion	100mg, 150mg, and 200mg up to 400mg
Wellbutrin XL	Bupropion	150mg and 300mg up to 450mg

Serotonin and norepinephrine reuptake inhibitors (SNRIs) are another newer form of antidepressant medication. These medications treat depression by increasing availability of both serotonin and norepinephrine.

The following are the more common SNRIs prescribed.

Table 10.C SNRI Medications

Brand Name	Generic Name	Dose Range up to Maximum Daily Dose
Cymbalta	Duloxetine	20mg, 30mg, and 60mg up to 120mg
Effexor	Venlafaxine	25mg, 37.5mg, 50mg, 75mg, and 100mg up to 375mg
Effexor XR	Venlafaxine	37.5mg, 75mg, and 150mg up to 225mg
Pristiq	Desvenlafaxine	50mg and 100mg up to 100mg
Remeron	Mirtazapine	15mg, 30mg, and 45mg up to 45mg

Selective serotonin reuptake inhibitors (SSRIs) are a newer form of antidepressant medication. These medications work by altering the amount of serotonin available in the brain.

The following include the more common SSRIs prescribed.

Table 10.D SSRI Medications

Brand Name	Generic name	Dose Range up to Maximum Daily Dose
Celexa	Citalopram	10mg, 20mg, and 40mg, up to 60mg
Lexapro	Escitalopram	5mg, 10mg, and 20mg up to 20mg
Paxil	Paroxetine	10mg, 20mg, 30mg, and 40mg up to 60mg
Paxil CR	Paroxetine	12.5mg, 25mg, up to 75mg
Prozac	Fluoxetine	10mg, 20mg, and 40mg up to 40mg
*Zoloft	Sertraline	25mg, 50mg, and 100mg up to 200mg

Tricyclic antidepressants (TCAs) were some of the first types to be used to treat depression. TCAs work specifically by affecting the levels of norepinephrine and serotonin in the brain. Although these drugs are effective in treating depression, they tend to have more side effects. Newer antidepressants, which have fewer side effects, tend to be tried first.

The following include the more common TCAs prescribed.

Table 10.E TCA Medications

Brand Name	Generic Name	Dose Range up to Maximum Daily Dose
*Anafranil	Clomipramine	25mg, 50mg, and 75mg up to 250mg
Asendin	Amoxapine	25mg, 50mg, 100mg, and 150mg up to 600mg
Elavil	Amitriptyline	25mg, 50mg, and 100 mg up to 300mg
*Norpramin	Desipramine	5mg, 10mg, 25mg, 50mg, 75mg, 100mg, and 150mg up to 300mg
Pamelor	Nortriptyline	10mg, 25mg, 50mg, and 75mg up to 150mg
Sinequan	Doxepin	10mg, 25mg, 50mg, 75mg, 100mg, and 150mg up to 300mg
Tofranil	Imipramine	10mg, 25mg, 50mg, 75mg, 100mg, and 150mg up to 300mg

Sometimes you may have what is known as treatment-resistant depression. This can be hard to diagnose. Sometimes people are diagnosed with depression but really have another disorder such as Bipolar Disorder or Dysthymia. Make sure other conditions such as a medical condition or substance abuse are ruled out as the causes of your depression. Also, if you have been diagnosed with depression, make sure you have been taking your medication as prescribed. People will often stop taking a medication because of a side effect. Some medications take up to twelve weeks to take effect. Sometimes people will have trouble taking their medications consistently. It is important to establish and follow a routine that will help you follow your medication treatment as prescribed by your psychiatrist.

If you have done all these things and the depression is still not lifting, perhaps switching or adding another medication should be tried. Sometimes your psychiatrist will add another medication not specifically geared for treating depression such as an anti-anxiety medicine or anti-convulsant or antipsychotic medicine. Now you might be thinking, *I'm not psychotic, and I don't have seizures. Why would I be prescribed an anticonvulsant or an antipsychotic medication?* These medicines are often used to treat specific symptoms that are not going away or being managed very well by the other medications you have been prescribed for the depression. For example, you might still be struggling with racing thoughts or trouble sleeping. If so, medications for sleep might be added. As you read in the chapter on sleep and eating, sleep is an essential part of overall mental and physical health.

Below is a list of other medications that might also be used in treating depression or treatment-resistant depression.

Table 10.F Other Medications Possibly Prescribed

Brand Name	Generic Name	Typical Symptoms Being Treated	Dose Range up to Maximum Daily Dose
*Abilify	Aripiprazole	Depressed mood, poor concentration	2mg, 5mg, 10mg, 15mg, 20mg, and 30mg, up to 30mg
Ambien	Zolipidem	Insomnia	5mg, and 10mg up to 10mg
Ambien CR	Zolipidem	Insomnia	6.25mg and 12.5mg up to 12.5mg
Ativan	Lorazepam	Anxiety	0.5mg, 1mg and 2mg up to 10mg
Buspar	Buspirone	Anxiety	5mg, 10mg, 15mg, and 30mg, up to 60mg
Depakote Depakote ER	Divalproex Sodium Divalproex Sodium ER	Mood stabilization, mania, irritability	125mg, 250mg, and 500mg
Equetro	Carbamazepine	Mood stabilization, depressed mood	100mg, 200mg, and 300mg up to 1600mg
Geodon	Ziprasidone	Mood stabilization, psychosis	20mg, 40mg, 60mg, and 80mg up to 200mg
Lamictal	Lamotrigine	Depressed mood, mood stabilization	25mg, 100mg, 150mg, and 200mg up to 200mg
Librium	Chlordiazepoxide	Anxiety and alcohol detoxification	5mg, 10mg, and 25mg up to 100mg
*Lithium	Lithium Carbonate	Mood stabilization, mania	150mg, 300mg, and 600mg up to 2400mg
*Lithobid	Lithium Carbonate ER	Mood stabilization, mania	300mg and 450mg, up to 1800mg

Lunesta	Eszopclone	Insomnia	1mg, 2mg, and 3mg up to 3mg
Rozerem	Ramelteon	Insomnia	8mg up to 8mg
Restoril	Temazepam	Insomnia	7.5mg, 15mg and 30mg up to 30mg
*Risperdal	Risperidone	Racing thoughts, mania, insomnia	0.25mg, 0.5mg, 1mg, 2mg, 3mg and 4mg up to 16mg
Seroquel	Quetiapine	Racing thoughts, insomnia, mania and depressed mood	25mg, 50mg, 100mg, 200mg, 300mg and 400mg up to 800mg
Seroquel XR	Quetiapine	Racing thoughts, insomnia, mania and depressed mood – to augment antidepressant	50mg, 150mg, 200mg, 300mg and 400mg up to 800mg
Symbyax	Fluoxetine/Olanzapine	Treatment Resistant Depression	Fixed ratio combination 3/25mg, 6/25mg, 6/50mg, 12/25mg, and 12/50mg up to 12/50mg
Valium	Diazepam	Anxiety, insomnia	2mg, 5mg and 10mg up to 10mg
Xanax	Alprazolam	Anxiety, panic attacks	0.25mg, 0.5mg, 1mg, and 2mg up to 4mg
Zyprexa	Olanzapine	Racing thoughts, insomnia, mania, dysphoria, hallucinations	2.5mg, 5mg, 7.5mg, 10mg, 15mg, and 20mg up to 20mg

*Indicates approved by the FDA for children

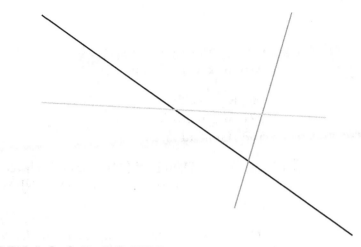

BIBLIOGRAPHY

American Psychiatric Association (2000). Diagnostic and statistical manual of mental disorders (4th Ed.–TR). Washington, D.C.: Author.

Baucom, D., Sayer, S. & Scher, T. (1990) Supplementary behavioral marital therapy with cognitive restructuring and emotional expressiveness training: An outcome investigation. Journal of Consulting and Clinical Psychology, 58, 636–645.

Beck, A.T. (1976). Cognitive therapy and the emotional disorders. New York: International Universities Press.

Beck, A. T., Rush, A. J., Shaw, B. F., & Emery, G. (1979). Cognitive therapy of depression. New York: Guilford Press.

Beck, J. S. (1995). Cognitive therapy: Basics and beyond. New York: Guilford Press.

Bedrosian, R. C. & Bozicas, G.D. (1994). Treating family of origin problems: A cognitive approach. New York: Guilford Press.

Bevilacqua, L. and Dattilio, F. (2010) Brief family therapy homework planner (2nd Ed.). Hoboken, NJ: Wiley & Sons.

Butler, G., Fennell, M., Robson, D., & Gelder, M. (1991). Comparison of behavior therapy and cognitive-behavior therapy in the treatment of generalized anxiety disorder. Journal of Consulting and Clinical Psychology, 59, 167–1754.

Dattilio, F. M. (1989). A guide to cognitive marital therapy. In P.A. Keller & S.R. Heyman (Eds.), Innovations in clinical practice: A source book (Vol. 8, pp.27–42). Sarasota, FL: Professional Resource Exchange.

Dattilio, F. M., & Padesky, C. A. (1990) Cognitive therapy with couples. Sarasota FL: Professional Research Exchange.

Dobson, K.S. (1989). A meta-analysis of the efficacy of cognitive therapy for depression. Journal of Consulting and Clinical Psychology, 57, 414–419.

Fairburn, C.G., Jones, R., Peveler, R.C., Hope, R.A., & Doll, H.A. (1991). Three psychological treatments for bulimia nervosa: A comparative trial. Archives of General Psychiatry, 48, 463–469.

Freeman, A. & DeWolf, R. (1990). Woulda, coulda, shoulda: Overcoming regrets, mistakes and missed opportunities. New York: Harper Collins Publishers.

Gelernter, C.S., Uhde, T.W., Cimbolic, P., Arnkoff, D.B., Vittone, B.J., Tancer, M.E. & Bartko, J.J. (1991). Cognitive-behavioral and pharmacological treatments of social phobia: A controlled study. Archives of General Psychiatry, 48, 938–945.

Salkovskis, p.m., Kirk, J. (1989). Obsessional disorders. In K. Hawton, Pm.M. Salkovskis, J. Kirk, & D.M. Clark (Eds.) Cognitive-behavior therapy for psychiatric problems: A practical guide (pp. 129–168). New York: Oxford University Press.

Woody, G.E., Luborsky, L., McClellan, A.T., O'Brien, C.P., Beck, A.T., Blaine, J., Herman, I., & Hole, A. (1983). Psychotherapy for opiate addicts: Does it help? Archives of General Psychiatry, 40, 1081–1086.

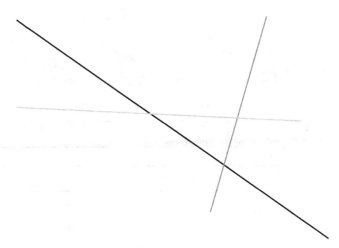

APPENDIX A:
LIFE COUNSELING SERVICES (LCS)
DEPRESSION SCREENING

Life Counseling Services Depression Screening

Name: _____   Counselor : _____

Male / Female   Age: _____   Date : _____

Please check the appropriate response as it relates to the past two weeks:

	Never or Rarely (0)	Sometimes (1)	Often (2)	Almost all the time (3)
I feel sad				
I feel like a failure				
I have lost interest in my work				
I do not look forward to the future				
I feel guilty				
I have lost interest in my hobbies				
I feel that others don't like me				
I am unhappy with myself				
I doubt my own judgment				
I am easily frustrated				
I wish I were dead				
I feel lonely				
I avoid being around other people				
My eating patterns have changed over the past month, such as overeating, or loss of appetite				
Total Page 1	-0-			

	Never or Rarely (0)	Sometimes (1)	Ofte (2)	Almost all the time (3)
I have suicidal thoughts				
I deserve to be punished				
I have difficulty making decisions				
I feel worn out				
I feel emotionally shut down				
I feel worthless				
I am not interested in sex				
I feel hopeless				
I blame myself for other people's problems				
I feel spiritually dead				
I have difficulty paying attention				
Pg. 1 Total	-0-			
Pg. 2 Total	-0-			
Total Score	-0-			

Sum of Total Scores: _____

Scoring

    1-20   Not depressed to Mild
    20-30 Mild to Moderate
    30 +   Moderate to Severe

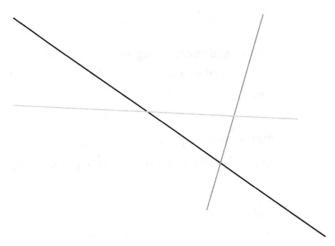

APPENDIX B:
DEPRESSION DIAGNOSES

The following stories are designed to give you some direction in understanding your symptoms. Though there are more disorders in the depression family, the examples below are the most common, and the examples below should help you visualize the range and severity of the symptoms that can accompany these disorders in everyday life.

It is not advised that depression should (or can) be diagnosed by reading a story. For example, Major Depressive Disorder may look very different from the example below depending on the person. Therefore, these stories are not an accurate way to diagnose your own symptoms of depression. If you are interested in receiving a formal diagnosis, a licensed mental health professional or a qualified medical doctor such as a psychiatrist should conduct it.

MINDY:
ADJUSTMENT DISORDER WITH DEPRESSED MOOD

Mindy lived in her childhood home for forty-five years, and it just sold. With her parents deceased for eight years now, she saw no good reason to live anywhere else. But the old house began to show wear, and each new problem became more costly to fix. Mindy, with encouragement from her brothers, reluctantly agreed to sell the house and move to an apartment closer to town and her job.

With her home on the market, Mindy felt all right until the day she received the news that the house had sold. Over the next month, she began to experience bouts of intense sadness while she packed up the house. After the move, her sadness became worse.

She cried in her apartment while she mulled over how terrible her new situation was, which just made her feel sadder and more discouraged. Mindy did not feel like doing much of anything at home, including unpacking and decorating her new place, cooking or watching television—all activities she used to enjoy. She dodged phone calls from friends and made excuses to avoid get-togethers. Once-weekly family dinners with her brothers became less frequent. Her energy in the evenings was poor, and she felt she had to drag herself to do anything. Surprisingly, as unenergetic as she felt, falling asleep sometimes took up to an hour, and she felt tired in the mornings.

Thankfully, work was her solace. Even though she didn't feel as energetic and enthusiastic about her job as in the past, being at work offered her peace from the sadness she felt at her new apartment. Work kept her interest. She socialized with coworkers and continued to meet the demands of the job, despite how she felt at home.

Understanding Mindy's symptoms:

- Leaving her childhood home to live in an unfamiliar surrounding was a clear *stressor* for Mindy.

- Mindy developed strong *emotional and behavioral symptoms* (i.e. sadness, low energy, crying, avoiding friends and family, not doing things she had enjoyed in the past) *within three months* of the start of the stressor.

- Mindy's *reaction* to the stressor of moving was *not typical* of the reaction that would be expected of others in the same situation.

- Her *symptoms interfered with* her usual *functioning* (i.e. she stopped spending time with friends and family).

- She *does not meet criteria for any disorder in the depression family.*

- Mindy's *symptoms were not* a reaction to the death of someone close to her (i.e. *bereavement*).

WILLIAM: MAJOR DEPRESSIVE DISORDER

William worked for the bank downtown as long as he could remember. He started as a bank teller when he was young and eventually worked his way to branch manager, a position he held for sixteen years. About ten months ago, the bank was bought out and new staff was brought in—William was laid off. This was the first time William had ever lost his job, and he was devastated. Shortly after, he began to feel depressed.

Over the next six months, he was sad most of the time, no matter what he was doing. Even spending time with his children and working on home improvement projects—his favorite activities in the past—gave him no pleasure. He lost interest in watching baseball, something he had done since he was twelve years old. Searching for jobs was difficult in the beginning, but he pushed through. Now just the thought made him feel completely overwhelmed, and he abandoned the idea all together. He had thoughts like, *Why bother? No one would want to hire me anyway* and *Things will never get better for me.*

William plummeted into the blackness of depression. He could not recall the last time he felt hungry, and his wife commented on his visible weight loss. William hadn't noticed because he was not dressing or caring for himself the way he used to. His days and nights consisted of lying exhausted in bed or watching television on the couch. Ironically, his sleep at night was erratic; some nights he could not fall asleep, and other nights he would wake five or six times a night worrying about finances or feeling guilty for not being able to provide for his wife and children. Repeatedly, William's mind wandered to thoughts about his life insurance policy and then to the thought that his family would be better off without him.

I'm just a burden to everybody, he said to himself. Occasionally, while driving, William imagined himself veering off the road into a tree. *All this pain would be gone then,* he thought.

Understanding William's symptoms:

- This is William's *first experience with depression* (Recurrent Major Depression would include at least two distinct episodes like this in a person's life).

- William's *mood* has been *depressed* for *more* time *than* it was *not* for a *minimum* of *two weeks.*

- He has a number of *symptoms,* including *depressed mood, poor appetite and weight loss, poor sleep, low energy, and negative thoughts about himself, the world, and the future.*

- William has recurrent thoughts about *suicide* or *death.*

- William is *clearly impaired in more than one area of his life* (i.e. both at home and socially and his symptoms interfere with his ability to find a new job).

- He was *not recently bereaved or abusing alcohol or drugs*. William has been seen by his family doctor and *does not have any medical condition* that might contribute to his symptoms.

CATHY: BIPOLAR I DISORDER

Cathy couldn't get over how great she felt sitting at the Philadelphia airport bar on Tuesday night. She was the life of the party and just added another round for the bar to her bar tab, which was three hundred dollars. Her euphoric feelings were even more noticeable given her strong depression over the past eight months. During that time, she spent a considerable number of days hopeless, sad, and in bed. But the past two weeks had been incredible. She hadn't slept for more than an hour a night, despite being at clubs and bars most of the time— Cathy just seemed to have limitless amounts of energy.

Recently, Cathy reconnected with Eric through a popular social networking website. Eric was her high school boyfriend whom she had not spoken to in twelve years, and they talked via e-mail for about an hour. Afterward, Cathy decided to surprise Eric in Cincinnati. She didn't know exactly where he lived, but she could figure all of that out when she landed. Eric and his new wife would be so excited to see her and definitely wouldn't mind her staying with them for a few days. It would be so much fun.

On the plane, Cathy talked continuously to passengers around her about her new job as a financial analyst and how she would probably be running the company soon due to her ability to accurately predict shifts in global markets—a special talent others just didn't have. It was hard for anyone to get a word in given how fast she talked and how quickly the topic changed, which made for an awkward atmosphere.

She ordered some needed items from the *Sky Depot* shopping catalogue, including two travel alarm clocks, nine pet cages (she planned to start a non-profit animal rescue after the trip), one hundred and fifty dollars of toddler clothing (despite not having children), an eight-hundred-dollar watch, and a "never, never, never give up" necklace for her fiancé, Pete. Pete had been worried about Cathy over the past week, but she was convinced he was just jealous of how good she was feeling. In fact, most of her family and friends were worried about her, and it really pissed her off when they brought it up. They just wanted to bring her down. *How could there be anything wrong with feeling so good?* she told herself.

Understanding Cathy's symptoms:

- Cathy's *mood* would be described as *euphoric.*

- She has a number of *symptoms* that are common during a manic episode, including: (a) dramatically *decreased* need for *sleep,* (b) *exaggerated self-confidence,* (c) *irritability,* (d) severely *compromised judgment,* (e) feeling *pressure to talk,* (f) *talking* very *quickly,* (g) *risky behaviors* (e.g. spending money, drug and alcohol abuse, promiscuity), and (h) *unusual thoughts, beliefs, or perceptual experiences* (i.e. belief that she has special abilities at work).

- She has *experienced* these symptoms for *at least one week.*

- Cathy is *clearly impaired.* Her spontaneous, mid-week trip to Cincinnati will likely interfere with her job when she fails to show up to work. Moreover, flying to see an ex-boyfriend will likely further strain her relationship with her fiancé, Pete. Her behavior is deeply troubling to her friends and family. Her erratic spending will result in a significant amount of debt she cannot afford.

- She is *not suffering from a general medical condition or using substances that would cause or better explain her symptoms.*

MEGAN: BIPOLAR II DISORDER

"In the last week, my mind is really working, and the ideas are flowing again," Megan told her boyfriend. Her voice was shaky and full of energy. She had always been creative, but the depressed times really got in the way. Now she was having great ideas again. Over the next four months her graphic design business flourished, and her ability to feel rested and energetic after three or four hours of sleep allowed her to take on more clients and produce more work—some of the finest in the graphic arts field, she thought. Despite the heavy workload, her projects got finished on time.

In fact, work pretty much consumed Megan. She talked about her ideas and the business most of the time with her boyfriend of six years, who was used to Megan's "creative periods" by now. He much preferred these creative periods to the depressed times she had experienced in the past. Sometimes, though, he worried that she might be taking on too much work and that when her creative period ended (it always did) she might be left feeling overwhelmed by the amount of work she had. However, Megan's inflated self-confidence and optimism made it hard for her to see his point. Instead, she viewed his concerns as "just more negativity" that was holding her back.

Understanding Megan's symptoms:

- Megan's *mood* would be described as *euphoric.*

- Megan has had *at least one* past *episode of Major Depression* and has *never had a full manic episode* (see Cathy's story).

- Megan is *talking faster than normal,* but she has the ability to have a shared conversation and tolerate being interrupted by others.

- She shows an *inflated sense of self-esteem* (i.e. about the quality of her work).

- She feels *very energetic* with *little sleep* and her energy is very *goal-directed* (i.e. work).

- Megan shows signs of *impaired judgment* (i.e. how much work she is taking on without appraising the consequences down the line); however, her judgment is not so impaired that it interferes significantly with follow-through on her projects.

- She has had the *symptoms* for *at least four days*.

- Megan's symptoms cannot be better explained by any other disorder.

The major difference between Bipolar I (see Cathy) and II (see Megan) is the degree of intensity and level of impairment during the elevated mood states (i.e. mania and hypomania) of the disorder. Both women have had past experiences with major depression, but their elevated mood states are distinctly different, with Cathy's mania being more severe and interfering much more significantly with her functioning than Megan's. In fact, Megan's energy levels and goal-directed activity actually fuel a very productive period in her job. Cathy's energy levels, on the other hand, are more distracting and interfere with productive behavior. Though Cathy's behavior may be goal-directed, her energy levels typically interfere with her ability to see ideas or projects through to completion. Her perception of her own abilities is also grossly exaggerated, which leads to severe problems with judgment (i.e. going to start a non-profit business or run a financial institution because of a perceived special ability).

DON: DYSTHYMIC DISORDER

Most of his life, Don had felt chronically unhappy. He just thought he was born that way. As long as he could remember, he never enjoyed life like other people. The birth of his son brought momentary happiness, but he quickly returned to his dreary state. There were only a handful of times in his life when Don felt happy for more than a few weeks. *I guess this is just another way I'm not good enough,* he told himself.

His energy wasn't good enough either, and no matter how much sleep he got, he always felt tired, which made it hard to concentrate at work. Despite having a good job at an information technology firm, Don was consumed by the belief that he was a failure at his job. His very low self-esteem gave way to poor motivation and low ambition, and he had never advanced at the company in his fifteen-year tenure, despite offers to do so. Coworkers gossiped that Don was nice, but that his negativity made him difficult to be around. "Let's face it," he'd say with all seriousness, "life's hard, and then you die."

Understanding Don's symptoms:

- Don had a number of symptoms characteristic of Dysthymic Disorder, including
  (a) increased *appetite*, (b) chronic *fatigue*,
  (c) *very low self-esteem*, (d) *problems with
  concentration* and (e) a persistently *hopeless*
  attitude.

- His *symptoms* had been there *more* often *than not* for *at least two years*. It is common that people with Dysthymia do not recognize their symptoms as a form of depression. Don had these symptoms for so long, it never occurred to him he might be depressed. Instead, he believed it was just how he was born.

- Don *hadn't experienced a Major Depressive Episode* (see William's story) *in the first two years* of his symptoms.

- He has *never had* a *manic* or *hypomanic episode* (see stories of Cathy and Megan).

- His *symptoms cannot be better explained* by another disorder, a general medical condition or drug or alcohol abuse.

- Don is *clearly impaired*. His symptoms affect him at home, socially and at work.

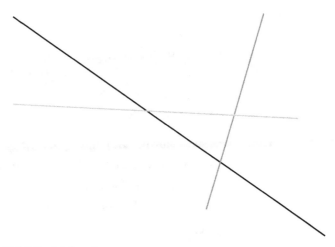

APPENDIX C:
HOW TO RELAX

DEEP BREATHING

- Lie down in your bed or sit in a comfortable (not too comfortable) chair and close your eyes.

- Put one hand on your stomach and one hand on your chest

- Take a slow deep breath in through your nose.

- Inhale deeply so that you feel the air going into your stomach.

- Picture a balloon in your stomach, which

you will be inflating with each inhale. If the hand on your chest is moving and the hand on your stomach is not, you are not breathing in deep enough.

- Exhale slowly through your mouth. Pretend that you are blowing out a candle. You could picture ten individual candles in front of you. With each exhale blow out one candle.

- With each exhale you may want to repeat a calming statement to yourself (e.g. I am tired, I am calm, I am relaxed, etc.).

PROGRESSIVE MUSCLE RELAXATION

1. Sit in a comfortable chair.

2. Slow down your breathing by breathing in through your nose and out through your mouth.

3. Tense each muscle group in your body for ten seconds (legs, abdomen, chest, shoulders).

4. After tensing each muscle group relax for ten to fifteen seconds.

Notice the difference in feeling tense and feeling relaxed.

GUIDED IMAGERY AND VISUALIZATION

Another way to decrease stress through relaxation is to use guided imagery and visualization. This essentially involves using deep breathing and pairing it with a visual image. You can also picture the tension or stress you have and replace it with an image of relaxation. For example, some of us feel stress and can picture a rope tied in a knot. Other people might picture a weight on their chest or the world on their shoulders. A relaxing alternative picture would be the rope loosening and coming unknotted or the weight being lifted like a balloon off of your chest or shoulders.

You can create any relaxing scene by using the following steps:

1. Sit in a comfortable chair.

2. Slow down your breathing by breathing in through your nose and out through your mouth.

3. Imagine the tense image (knotted rope or weight on your chest).

4. Imagine the image being transformed.

For step four, use as much vivid detail as possible. Try to feel the tension leaving your body as you imagine the image changing. The rope is loosening, and the knot is coming untied. As it is loosening, so is your tension. You can also repeat to yourself, "I'm relaxing" or "I'm feeling calmer." With each exhale imagine the tension leaving your body and feeling more relaxed. You can also imagine breathing away your tension. As you breathe out, imagine your breath blowing away a sailboat. As the boat sets sail and moves farther and farther out of view, so is your tension. Try to create your own image. Perhaps have a few different images to choose from. You may want to write out the scene and record it on a digital recorder. If you don't like hearing your own voice there are many relaxation CDs available at bookstores and online for you to try out as you use visualization.

PAMPER YOURSELF WITH BUBBLES

In today's busy world, most of us don't set aside time for ourselves. If you decide to plan some "me time," a great way to pamper yourself and relax and unwind is to take a bubble bath. Make sure you plan this out. Oftentimes I hear, "Oh, I tried that, and I had fifteen knocks at the door before I even got in the tub." Plan your experience.

1. Privacy! If you can't get everyone to leave you alone for an hour, you might have to wait until everyone else goes to bed.

2. Setting the mood. Get some soft and relaxing music to listen to while soaking your cares away. (Be sure to keep any electronics away from the bathtub.)

3. Lighting. You can use some lavender scented candles or just dim the lights.

4. The bubbles. Use some scented bubbles. Some skin-moisturizing oils can also add to your experience.

5. The after bath moisturizer. Once you get toweled off try rubbing on some conditioning cream.

Now you are ready to sleep! Good night.

Thanks for reading, *When You Can't Snap Out of it: The Journey Through Depression*. I hope you found the ideas helpful and more importantly effective. Remember, you are not alone. You can learn to manage and overcome depression. There is hope for healing.

Feel free to visit Dr. Lou at his website at
www.drlouonline.com